D0439551

Ready, Set,
READ!

Ready, Set, READ!

A Start-to-Finish Reading Program Any Parent Can Use

BARBARA CURTIS

BROADMAN
& HOLMAN
PUBLISHERS

Nashville, Tennessee

© 1998
by Barbara Curtis
All rights reserved
Printed in the United States of America

0-8054-0167-9

Published by Broadman & Holman Publishers, Nashville, Tennessee
Page Design: Sam Gantt Graphic Design Group
Acquisitions Editor: Vicki Crumpton
Page Composition: Desktop Miracles, Dallas, Texas

Dewey Decimal Classification: 372.41
Subject Heading: READING (EARLY CHILDHOOD) / READING—
PARENT PARTICIPATI0N / READING—PHONETIC METHOD
Library of Congress Card Catalog Number: 98-12865

Unless otherwise stated all Scripture citation is from the NIV, the Holy
Bible, New International Version, copyright © 1973, 1978, 1984 by
International Bible Society. Other versions cited are New King James
Version, copyright © 1979, 1980, 1982, Thomas Nelson, Inc., Publishers;
and KJV, the King James Version.

Library of Congress Cataloging-in-Publication Data

Curtis, Barbara, 1948–
    Read, set, read : a start-to-finish reading program any parent can use /
Barbara Curtis
       p.   cm.
    Includes bibliographical references.
    ISBN 0-8054-0167-9 (pbk)
    1. Reading (Early childhood).   2. Reading—Parent participation.
3. Reading—Phonetic method.   4. Children—Books and reading
LB1139.5.R43C87   1998
372.41—dc21

                                                              98-12865
                                                              CIP

1 2 3 4 5 02 01 00 99 98

For all the young mothers I know,
especially
Samantha, Mary, Laurie, Lisa,
Audrey, Trudie, Amy, Christine, Val,
Shampa, Karol, Jennifer, Stacey,
Nancy, Aydee, and Mimi.

With appreciation for all the mothers
who've passed this way before. And thanks to my
Maker for stretching me in between.

TITUS 2:4

Barbara Curtis is available for motivational speaking
engagements and workshops.
Contact her c/o Broadman & Holman
127 Ninth Avenue North
Nashville, TN 37234
E-mail: Ajointheir@aol.com

Contents

Acknowledgments

One of the greatest accomplishments of my life has been teaching children to read, as well as teaching parents to teach their children to read.

I am grateful to the Washington Montessori Institute, where I received my training, for equipping me with an approach to reading that worked so well for me as a teacher.

How wonderful later to find that this highly effective approach could work even more beautifully and smoothly at home! Today, as I spot my children lounging here and there throughout the house, each one caught up in a good book, I am even more satisfied knowing that I was responsible for teaching them to read.

Writing *Ready, Set, Read!* has given me the opportunity to extend all I've learned and taught—thus equipping more parents than ever with all they need to find that same sense of accomplishment and joy.

Thank you to my editor, Vicki Crumpton, as well as my publisher, Broadman and Holman, for catching my enthusiasm and making this dream possible.

Thanks to my wonderful and supportive family for sharing Mommy for a little while. After my first book, *Small*

Beginnings, except for my ever-encouraging husband Tripp, the main supporting cast for this book changed. Jasmine began working as the first official tour guide at Mrs. Grossman's sticker factory and will be married by the time this book is in your hands. Joshua went off to high school. Matthew and Zachary stepped into position as the number one helpers this time around. Way to go, boys!

Thanks to Rebecca Cain, "Grandma Becca" to my children, who faithfully devoted every Wednesday to spending time with all the little ones so I could write one day a week with complete serenity—knowing babies Jesse and Daniel were being taken for walks and having bubbles blown, and Sophia, Jonathan, and Madeleine were reading and being read to. As my son Benjamin said, "What a wonderful example for us all!"

Thanks to Donna McCornack for the many practical and tender things she did to help me through the six months of writing this book. And thanks to our dear friends Jim and Nancy Rehkopf for sharing some wonderful dinners and stimulating conversation.

Again, thanks to my spiritual parents, Dr. James Dobson and Dennis and Barbara Rainey. I will always be grateful that you were there when I was finally ready to hear.

Introduction

You can do it! You can teach your children to read. You can open the gateway to a rich, rewarding adventure that will beckon them on for the rest of their lives. You can set their feet on the path to a lifelong love of reading.

Through teaching your children yourself, in an informal and loving way, you can control the momentum, drawing them closer to reading at a pace tailored to their own individual needs. You can anticipate your children's trouble spots and give them extra encouragement when they need it, thus diverting feelings of inadequacy or failure, which make for unmotivated readers later on.

Your investment will build eagerness and self-confidence in each of your children, making every realm of knowledge as available as an open book. In addition, your involvement in his first efforts will nurture a love for words and ideas that will boost your child's potential for success—no matter where his future finds him.

Teaching your child to read may sound like a tall order for an ordinary parent. It isn't. Since the first hieroglyphics, most literate children learned to read at home, taught by their parents. This resulted in some charming and intimate teaching methods, as when Hebrew parents baked cakes in the form of letters of the Hebrew alphabet, requiring their children to name the letters before they ate the cakes. Parents wrote words with honey for the child to read and lick from a slate, that "the words of the law might be sweet on his lips."

Reading was not a compartmentalized task that one had to leave the home to learn, but part of the family bond—parents and older siblings passing on the keys that would unlock the secrets of the books the children had been hearing read aloud for as long as they could remember. Reading was part of a natural flow in the development of the child.

In the United States, two factors brought about a change:
1. The advent of public education—originally intended to extend literacy to every child
2. Our modern emphasis on specialization

Both factors have eroded parents' confidence in their abilities to teach their children anything—particularly reading skills. For decades we have left the most important part of our children's education to the "professionals," giving them credit for being better equipped to teach reading than we are.

But are they?

Consider the current state of affairs:

- A growing percentage of high school students graduate with inadequate reading skills.
- A president dramatically mandates that every child will read by third grade—despite the fact that almost everyone used to read in first.

- Colleges offer remedial courses for incoming freshmen who failed to master material formerly part of the core high school curriculum.
- Numerous, expensive reading programs sell like hotcakes to worried parents who sense their children just aren't where they should be in school.

It doesn't sound as though the "professionals" are better equipped at all!

That's because in the past few decades, public education has turned the reading realm upside down. "Educrats" (a term for educators in policy-making positions rather than teaching positions) seemingly arbitrarily replaced a consistently successful teaching method with something more modern: the "whole language" approach to reading. Now we are reaping the negative consequences of this failed experiment.

Didn't anyone notice that the traditional approach produced the desired results? Perhaps these educrats should have remembered the maxim, *If it works, don't fix it.*

PHONETICS FIRST

What worked in teaching reading was phonetics, plain and simple. Why? Because English—despite the variations we trip over and laugh about—is basically a phonetic language. Of some five hundred thousand words in the dictionary, 85 percent are phonetic.

Of course, there are exceptions. Think of *ough*. I come up with six ways to say it: *oo* in thr*ough*, *uff* in r*ough*, *off* in c*ough*, *au* in b*ough*t, *o* in th*ough*, and *ow* in b*ough*.

Obviously, words like these are learned only by sight. Sight recognition is part of any reading program.

But sight reading is a secondary approach, part of an arsenal professionals call *word attack skills*. Word attack skills include all the tools we give a child to master reading. Important as it is to conquer the exceptions in the English language, sight reading does not adequately replace a phonetic approach to reading.

You see, if a child is only taught to know words by sight, it may take him a lifetime to master 425,000 words (85 percent of the English language).

However, if a child learns to read phonetically, she has the tool to master most words and the confidence to pick up the other tools when needed.

The foundation of any valuable reading program, then, must be phonetics. A child who learns to read phonetically inherits a wealth of material available to practice his reading skills (see book recommendations in chapter 3 for early readers). As his confidence grows, his motivation increases. Memorizing sight words actually becomes easier.

Although the public school system has been slow to admit its error and return to the tried-and-true phonetic approach to reading, many others have caught on. And they're making a lot of money. The media is saturated with ads for programs like Hooked on Phonics and The Phonics Game. Many parents recognize that they need to take responsibility for something they used to take for granted as part of their children's away-from-home education.

You picked up *Ready, Set, Read!* because you are interested in your child's reading development. Maybe you want to teach her to read. Perhaps you want to improve his prereading skills before he begins the formal part of his education in public, private, or home school. Or maybe you just want an overview of the language process so you can better evaluate schools, curriculums, and teaching approaches.

Don't invest another dollar in reading materials before you've finished reading this book. You may be very surprised by how simple it actually is to produce an excellent and enthusiastic reader. The good news is you don't need to spend hundreds of dollars.

But the best news of all is that you can experience the enormous satisfaction of teaching your child one of the most important skills he'll ever learn. I wrote this book to put a simple, successful, and very affordable approach to reading in the hands of as many parents as possible.

I'm a parent myself—of eleven children. Perhaps it's the mother in me that accounts for my deep concern for the pressures and worries other parents face. God has given me a desire to unburden, enlighten, and encourage parents in any way I can. And he has given me some experience that enables me to do so.

ABOUT ME

As a new mother in 1970, I came across a book by Maria Montessori, *The Absorbent Mind.*[1] I was immediately fascinated, as I could see the truth in her observations about children. How could I doubt them when my own toddler Samantha was living proof?

Maria Montessori had a devotion to children I couldn't help but admire. She had an ability to see the world through the eyes of toddlers when the rest of the world was passing them by.

At the turn of the century, she became the first woman doctor in Italy. But her real life's mission was with children. Her work with children who had been labelled "retarded" (today called "developmentally delayed") led her to find ways to teach them reading and writing. She was so successful that these "retarded" children were soon outperforming their "normal" peers.

But what seemed miraculous to others was a source of great concern to her. If these disadvantaged children could do so well, what was keeping developmentally "normal" children on such a low level? Maria Montessori's great love for children and her belief in their potential motivated her to construct an educational method that would meet their needs at appropriate times.

I wanted to learn that method. Therefore I returned to college and eventually to the Washington Montessori Institute to become a teacher. In the decades since, I have taught in classrooms on both the east and west coasts, in the inner city and suburbia, with children of all ethnic groups and social strata.

What's more, I eventually became a mother many times over. Samantha is now grown with three children of her own, and my second daughter, Jasmine, will soon be married as well. By a stroke of God's grace, thirteen years after my first child was born and eight years after my second, I finally realized my true calling. In addition to my two adult daughters,

I now have nine children under age fifteen (the last two we've adopted).

In *Small Beginnings: First Steps to Prepare Your Child for Lifelong Learning*, I shared many Montessori-based ideas, tested and refined during my own twenty-eight years of motherhood and six years of home schooling. For anyone reading *Ready, Set, Read!*, I recommend my first book as well. It will teach you how to encourage qualities that will prepare your child for *any* kind of learning: qualities such as independence, concentration, a sense of order, and self-control. *Small Beginnings* also outlines exercises that lead into pre-reading skills: hand-eye coordination, pincerlike grasp for writing, and left to right sequencing.

As in *Small Beginnings*, my purpose in *Ready, Set, Read!* is:

- to dispel the mystique of professionalism that surrounds teaching young children,
- to share knowledge of the child's God-given potential for learning,
- to help parents discover their own potential as teachers,
- to empower parents to lay a foundation of joyful, lifelong learning (in this book, more specifically, reading) on which their children can build—in public, private, and home schools.

WHY AN EARLY START?

All my years with children—as a teacher and a mother— have confirmed what I originally learned from a book; the first five years of a child's life involve a period of intense absorption and learning. God has built into each child the potential for seeking knowledge.

Look closely at children's activities and you will see a sense of purposefulness, working toward understanding and mastering their small worlds. Maria Montessori noticed that slum children, who had no toys of their own, found crumbs of bread on the ground to examine and play with. What a testimony to these children's relentless drive to explore and learn about their environment!

More and more experts are zeroing in on the toddler years. In the spring of 1997, Oprah Winfrey devoted a show to the importance of the toddler years. *Newsweek* magazine published a special issue called *Your Child* including articles such as "How to Build a Baby's Brain." There is a growing realization that the majority of learning takes place before children enter kindergarten. That's when the child's drive to learn is strongest.

God gives the child this drive to explore and learn. You see it clearly in the toddler years: *learning is what we are made for*. It is our drive to learn that causes us to seek to know more about God and the world he created for us. Watch any preschooler learning to peel carrots, write his name, or count his pennies, and you will see a child completely engrossed, a child who isn't learning because he *has* to, but because he *wants* to—a child who loves to learn.

What happens, then, that produces older children who are bored and blasé, reluctant to learn? Maria Montessori, and now many modern experts, would say that these children probably began learning too late, and therefore lost their potential love of learning.

Montessori's idea was that the child has sensitive periods for learning—times when areas of knowledge can be acquired effortlessly if the conditions are right. The right conditions include age-appropriate environmental cues, plus loving parents or teachers who understand the child's needs and try to steer her course in the right direction.

When we wait too long to teach children certain skills, they learn with more difficulty and less joy. When we help our children learn the appropriate skills at the appropriate times, learning takes place without strain, is enjoyable, and leads to the desire to learn more—thus creating a lifelong love of learning.

I believe this is what God intended for our children.

What parent doesn't want each child to reach his potential? And what parent wouldn't choose to make the learning process as filled with joy and satisfaction as possible? To be good stewards of what God has given us, we parents need to know when the best time is for our children to learn and what tools we need to give them.

THE SENSITIVE PERIOD FOR READING

The sensitive period for reading, according to Montessori and confirmed by my own teaching experience, is before the age of six. I know that some educators argue otherwise, but perhaps they have not been using a method tailored to match the needs of young children. Young children learn differently from elementary age children. Because Montessori understood children so well, the method she devised for teaching reading is tailored to meet those needs. Most young children who are taught in the sequence you will find in chapter 2 will be reading before they begin their formal education, wherever that may be.

I say "most young children" because there are exceptions. Some children just seem to be born with different timetables. I've experienced this firsthand in my own home. After twenty-five years of teaching preschoolers to read, I had the toughest time with my daughter Sophia.

Sophia finally learned to read in December 1996 at the age of seven, though I had used the same approach with her since the age of three. A "normal" child in every way, she seemed to run on a different clock in this one area. I think God wanted me to see—before I wrote this book—what a wide range of variation he has allowed.

I must admit there were times when I almost gave up on Sophia. If you find yourself in this position, don't give up. Once Sophia began barely sounding out three-letter phonetic words, she was so happy with her new ability that she kept pushing herself. Within six months she was reading at second-grade level and regaling her family with riddles from *Clubhouse Jr.* magazine (see appendix A).

All by way of saying, an approach is just that, an approach. It's not a strait jacket. A child's lack of immediate success should never lead to his feeling like a failure, nor to yours. Always encourage your child, keep trying, and keep praying.

Also, try not to judge your own efforts in terms of failure and success. Learning is a process. It takes as long as it takes. See appendix B for my list of favorite encouraging words.

How I See It

Most reading programs offer techniques for teaching reading as though it were a stand-alone skill, like sewing or carpentry.

But reading does not stand alone. It has deep roots. Reading is a natural extension of our human desire to communicate, which begins when a baby first babbles. On an individual level, the drive to communicate shapes and is shaped by the child's unique personality, ever expanding the ability to understand, express, evaluate, and form his or her own ideas.

The ability to read is in many ways dependent on the child's early experience of language. Evidence continues to accumulate supporting a direct relationship between early environments rich in language and a higher IQ.

When fifty-something Mortimer Zuckerman, editor-in-chief of *U. S. News and World Report*, had his first child in 1997, he devoted an entire back-page editorial to his concern for his daughter's future—rethinking the popular wisdom that quality time makes up for quantity time. Since recent studies indicate that most connections in the child's brain are laid down before the age of three, and since so much of that connecting is based on exposure to the spoken word, Zuckerman urged his readers to rethink their positions on day care. He came as close as he could to evangelizing for stay-at-home parents—someone to talk to their babies all day.

I agree with Zuckerman. In general, babies at home do get a head start in language. And babies who have a head start in language will have a head start in reading as well. Because I believe reading is best understood in the context of our whole language development, this book will begin at birth.

My hope is to inspire a greater appreciation for the miracle of language, to add a spiritual dimension as you teach your children to read.

THE SPIRITUAL ASPECT OF LANGUAGE

Language is a special gift from God. The first job he gave Adam was to name the animals. The ability to name and understand the things of our world is a distinctly human ability.

Language allows us to share information, ideas, and feelings. It enriches our relationships with others and with God.

The desire to communicate is obvious from the child's earliest months. Most children learn to speak without direct teaching. As long as everything in the environment is in order and the child is developmentally sound, he will pass certain milestones with no special effort on the parents' part. In chapter 1, we will see how children develop spoken language—from the first babbles to first words to first simple sentences.

This information can be of enormous benefit to you who want to get your children off to a good start. As parents, the more we understand about God's part in *every* aspect of our children's development, the more inspiration we will have to do our best. Partnering with God to release your child's potential is much easier than doing it alone. Through understanding God's design for your child's spoken language, you will be able to see how reading flows naturally from that. You will be better equipped and more confident in teaching your child to read.

In chapters 2 and 3 I will share a tried-and-true method of teaching children to read, using snatches of time and simple materials, in a way that fits in with everyday living.

And isn't this the way you want your child to feel about reading? Something warm and comfortable, part of his daily routine, not something reserved for a certain environment or for meeting specific assignments.

Each age-group section will also offer insights into choosing books for the child at each particular level—from board books to picture books, from read-aloud stories to the child's first readers. A child at each stage has certain needs, certain emotional concerns—and books are a way of meeting them.

In addition, books can be a bridge to great ideas and solid values. The best children's books have a subtext—a message behind the story—that communicates something in addition to the story itself. Just as Jesus used parables to teach the people of his time, authors use children's stories to teach children. Parents need to be aware of this so they can make sure that what they are reading enhances the values they are building at home. There is too much good reading material out there to waste time with anything second rate!

LET'S GET STARTED

I'm a firm believer in this: The best teachers love what they're doing. I've enjoyed teaching reading because I love to read myself. As a child I preferred reading to almost any other activity. As an adult I find books are my number one interest—after my family.

If that's the case with you, you're already off to a great start. If not, I'd like to suggest that you try to find a new interest or rekindle an old one in reading. If you never developed a love for books, it's never too late to give them another try. You may have a more enjoyable experience when you choose to re-read a classic that you once thought you hated because it was forced on you. One of my most rewarding experiences has been reading *David Copperfield* aloud to my children. My husband, Tripp, has read many classics to our children, night after night, chapter by chapter. As a result, their memories, vocabularies, and empathy for others have grown.

Remember, children learn best by example. That fact can be a powerful motivation for us to change when we see that by changing we can offer our children so much more. And God blesses our commitment to change for the sake of our children—sometimes he even makes it seem easy.

One of the wonderful gifts God gives us through our children is the chance to see things fresh and new. He uses them to shake us out of our old worn-out ideas and limitations.

For you, this may be the case with reading. Helping your child learn to read may awaken something in you. As you teach your child, you too may discover a lifelong love of reading.

Chapter One
READY
Birth to Two Years

*A*llison and Steve had waited longer than they wanted to start their family. By the time they felt financially ready and willing, Allison's body didn't cooperate right away. It took several years more to actually conceive. Perhaps this is why they treasured every moment of the pregnancy. At night after a stressful day at work, Steve loved to place his ear on Allison's ever-expanding tummy and listen to the sounds of his daughter—they knew it was a girl from the ultrasound! He imagined her turning watery somersaults, peacefully growing, waiting expectantly for the light. Holding Allison's hand, he'd almost envy the closeness of his wife and child, knowing that every word from Allison's lips must be sweet music to their baby's ears. Wanting to participate in these first special months with Tina (they'd decided to name her Bettina for his grandmother, but already called her Tina for short), her daddy would stroke Allison's so-soft-he-could-hardly-believe-it skin, bridging the small distance between him and his daughter by crooning old lullabies. Allison had shown him an article—from Newsweek, no less—that claimed babies could

hear "in utero." Somehow lullabies seemed like the way to go,
but Steve could hardly believe he remembered them!

COMFORT, COMMUNICATION, AND THE CREATOR

In the cozy closeness of the womb, a child is introduced to language—through his mother's voice, and in the best of circumstances, his father's. The effect of this early exposure is obvious from the start. Newborns are more sensitive to human sounds than any others.

In addition to responding more readily to human voices, they show a marked preference for the sounds with which they've grown familiar prenatally. Amazingly, infants are born with an ear for their native tongue: studies of four-day-old French babies found they responded more eagerly to French speakers than to Russian; for Russian babies, the opposite held true.

In the early days the voices of mother and father, brothers and sisters, grandmas and grandpas will surround the baby with love—and language. From the beginning, language is based on intimacy. Mothers and fathers coo and sing while holding their babies close and snuggling. They even speak a different language than they speak with co-workers or friends, what some experts have called "parentese."

Have you ever noticed how adults pitch their voices higher when talking to babies? People of every culture speaking every language use this method of "baby talk." We don't need to be told to do this; it happens almost instinctively. And there's a good reason for it. Studies prove that babies turn their attention more readily to high-pitched voices. In some unidentified way it's part of their preparation for human language.

> ## Language Development Begins in the Womb
> - Newborn infants show marked preferences
> - Babies are more responsive to human voices
> - Babies are more responsive to their native tongue
> - Babies are more responsive to their mothers' (and often fathers') voices
> - Babies are more responsive to higher-pitched voices

The origins of human language are still a mystery to many secular linguists. Far more complex than that of "other animals," human communication fascinates. These linguists wonder—but will never completely understand—why the child understands the concept of *dada*, then speaks it. They speculate on how children are able to pick up the rules of their native tongue with no formal instruction. Some theorize a "learning program" in the brain's structure to explain how humans arrived at such sophistication. Humans, they think, must have a genetically determined predisposition for language and language structure that is the result of the evolutionary process.

Yet something as intricate as language couldn't evolve spontaneously any more than one of Beethoven's symphonies or Duke Ellington's compositions could. There had to be a Grand Plan. *God gave us the gift of language.*

We need it. Animals have instincts that compel them toward the behavior appropriate to their species; how to hide from enemies, build nests, protect, feed, and care for their young, and teach their young to run or to fly.

Compare human infants with animal babies. Humans take almost a year to walk independently; horses walk and run within minutes of birth. In the animal kingdom, the young are helpless for only the briefest period and their own development is governed by instinct. All their instinctual behaviors would be released even if they were kept in a solitary condition.

Not so with humans. We don't have many instincts. We have potentials—given to us by God—that can only be released if certain requirements are met within our environment. Unlike animals, human infants are completely dependent on their parents for years. Most training is accomplished through language. The few documented cases of children who grew up apart from humans, as well as studies of children raised in isolated or solitary conditions, describe individuals with limited human characteristics. God must have had something in mind when he created us this way.

Consider how significant a role language plays in God's plan for us. Language is so essential—so intricately woven into our humanness—could we really be human without it? Not if you consider how clearly God made us not to be alone.

Through his gift of language, God provided a basis for his best gift of all—relationship. He designed us to be deeply involved in each other's lives, and language is the medium of interdependence. The warm communication between parent and baby sets the stage for the development of language. In the absence of serious deficiencies, the beginning of language takes place in the context of love.

This loving context is critical to the child's later ability to communicate and trust. The assurance of mother love is essential to the optimum development of language in the child.

It begins with the baby's first cry. Even in her first wail, a baby expresses her individuality. Neonatal nurses know firsthand that in hospital nurseries, each newborn has a distinctly personal cry. Mothers with many children will attest that their babies' voices varied in style, tone, and volume, each producing a unique cry.

Crying is the baby's first form of communication. Where does crying come from? The newborn's cry is really a reflex reaction to discomfort. The baby is hungry or hurting. The world is alerted. His parents respond.

The first few days after Allison and Steve brought Tina (yes, she really was a girl!) home from the hospital, she slept a lot. Then it seemed as though she had only two settings: sleeping and crying. Her sleepless parents had heard about some methods of scheduling that allowed babies to cry for long periods of time. But looking at their helpless baby and seeing her relief when she heard their voices and they held her close, the new parents felt only compassion. Somehow it seemed the right thing to do.

Baby's Speech and Language Development

Throughout the ages in diverse cultures, parents have responded unconditionally to babies' cries. In our own "sophisticated" culture, we sometimes wonder if that's the right thing to do, worrying that we'll spoil the baby. Perhaps we are a little too anxious to get back to an ordinary routine after an extraordinary event has taken place. Steve and Allison's decision to do what felt natural, to respond to their baby's cries, will set the stage for a trusting relationship and good communication between parents and child.

In the early months of a baby's life, this unconditional response is crucial. When a baby cries from hunger or hurt and no one responds, he will not learn that communication is effective. He may give up, become listless (the sign of a baby in despair), like the babies we see from countries where the food supply never filters down to the most helpless.

Through having needs met—hunger filled or comfort restored —the baby experiences communication as some-thing that brings closeness and contentment. This positive beginning is damaged when parents ignore their infant's cries for the sake of "discipline." Discipline will come later and, hopefully, by more positive means. During the early months, parents do well to pray for patience and for God to change their hearts to be able to accept their newborn's needs and "language" without reservation. They will reap the rewards later.

Body language is another big part of an infant's commu-nicational package. As he grows stronger, the baby uses every part of her body to "speak." She waves her arms and hands, wiggles her torso, thrusts her face forward, and turns toward or away from others. As she grows older, she signals wanting to be picked up, to be put down, or needing more space—wordlessly, but unmistakably.

Attachment Parenting Sets the Stage for Loving Communication

Parenting programs aimed at imposing early discipline through scheduled infant feedings and limited cuddling time interfere with the infant's proper development—particularly in the area of language. A crying infant needs to be fed, changed, or perhaps just held. Reassuring him gives positive reinforcement to the only form of communication he has.

Dr. William Sears and his wife, Martha, practicing pediatrician and pediatric nurse, authors of twenty-two books on child rearing, and—perhaps most importantly—Christian parents of eight children, advocate "attachment parenting"—creating a strong and loving bond between parent and infant. I recommend their comprehensive *Complete Book of Christian Parenting and Childcare* to get parents and babies off to the right start.

Meanwhile, the baby's cries become more differentiated, and our ears become more attuned, so that we begin to know if a cry means baby needs a feeding, a diaper change, comfort, or a nap. As we learn the baby's "language" and respond appropriately, she develops trust and confidence. Even in the earliest years, good communication builds stronger relationships.

The other side of parent–child communication consists of the parents' vocalizations as they feed, bathe, and dress the baby. Though these may seem one-sided—the parent talking *to* the infant—they are vital, laying an early foundation for language development.

At one month, Tina would stare intently at Allison as though her mother's "baby talk" were the most captivating show on earth. Allison felt more important than she'd ever felt in her life. It was beginning to feel as though they were really connecting. Not in the sense that they were not connected before, but as though there was a real conversation going on, even though Tina wasn't really making any noise.

Any witness to that intense look of an infant concentrating faithfully on the words his mom or dad is speaking knows something important is going on. The baby is learning to listen—the other side of communication and language skills.

Baby's first smile is really his first attempt to communicate back something positive. No intellectual analysis will convey more than the tremendous satisfaction a parent feels when receiving this coveted communication.

Cooing

Soon, the infant begins to seem aware—in between the uncomfortable and unhappy times—that there is another state of being—contentment. He begins to express his contentment. He coos. His communication potential expands, since his language is no longer limited to moments of discomfort but to expressing pleasure as well.

He feels contented; he makes noises of contentment. By at least occasionally responding to their baby's coos of contentment, as well as to cries of discontentment, parents help establish this positive side of communication in the child's early language. Again, communication builds relationship.

Clearly, God designed language as something that would shape, express, and enhance our relationships. And, miraculously, no matter how difficult his native tongue, only two conditions are necessary for a child anywhere in the world to learn language: (1) intimacy with others, and (2) language in the environment.

Most of the time these conditions are met without our even thinking about it. We take so much for granted—until we see some part of the process disrupted, as for instance in a handicapped, institutionalized, or economically disadvantaged child. Then we begin to appreciate that though countless children all over the world are cooing for the first time today, their numbers don't make it any less a miracle.

From that first coo, each child will arrive at adulthood with a vocabulary of twenty thousand to fifty thousand words and appropriate syntax (which we'll discuss later) for his particular language.

But that's a long look ahead. There's much more to accomplish before he gets there.

Allison was playing with Tina one day in the way they'd learned together. "Ah—boo!" Allison would say and bump her head lightly on Tina's tummy, brushing her hair across her daughter's face. Tina would squeal with delight. After several

bouts of ah-boos, a few tickles, and a good hug, Allison left Tina with some special toys to capture her attention. She knew it was good for Tina to have some time to play alone. This would pave the way to her independence later on. And it gave Allison a chance to catch up on her thank-you notes for all the baby gifts they'd received, including the special blanket Tina was playing on a few feet away from her mother's desk. Allison was trying to find the right words to describe her appreciation for the snowsuit they'd never need (her great-great aunt was a big believer in bundling babies to the max) when she heard something new: "babababa." The thank-you notes were promptly forgotten as Allison grabbed the phone to call Steve, her mother, and her best friend.

◆   ◆   ◆   ◆

Babababa—Babbling

At four to five months of age, the child enters the stage of language acquisition known as babbling (I have found it satisfying to know that even the experts use the same terms we do for the first two stages: cooing and babbling). Now the child begins to experiment with his lips and tongue to change the sounds he makes: babababa, mumumumu, gaga-gaga, dodododo.

The amazing aspect about this stage is that in random babbling the baby proves capable of producing *every* sound of *every* language.

So if at five months we are capable of reproducing every sound, why is it so hard in high school to pronounce the *u* in the French word *tu* (which my French teacher urged us to say properly by rounding our lips and saying *ee*—what a concept!). Or how about rolling *rrrr*'s in Spanish, *ch* as in the German *ich*, not to mention the intonations and (to Westerners) unusual sounds of Chinese, Japanese, and a host of Asian languages.

The unmistakable fact is that in acquiring our own language, we lose a lot. As the child plays and practices a huge repertoire of sounds, he begins to let go of some. He concentrates and holds on to only those sounds he hears in his environment, discarding those that are not part of his native language.

This is why, with no special effort, a child in a bilingual home can learn two languages and speak them fluently. For children, all languages are equally easy to learn. As adults, on the other hand, we find some languages easier to learn than others. It's not just the vocabulary and sentence structure that challenge us, but also these discarded phonemes (linguistic lingo for the sounds which are the building blocks of language). No matter how well we master, say Japanese, it's safe to say no one will mistake us for a native.

Still, though the words and even the basic sounds of each language are different, there are universal patterns followed by every child in acquiring his native tongue. No matter the culture or language, every able child follows the same developmental sequence.

Like most new parents, Allison and Steve were impatient for Tina's first word. But Allison's next-door neighbor Maria, who had three-year-old twin boys and a really cute eighteen-month-old

---

Language Milestones

4–6 weeks:	**smiling** (nonverbal communication)
2–4 months:	**cooing**
6–12 months:	**babbling** (undifferentiated sounds), followed by **deliberate mimicking**
1 year or so:	**single words**
2 years or so:	**two word utterances,** leading to **simple sentences**

---

daughter, said she'd have to wait a while. Maria told her it was important to name things, though, because babies learn to understand words before they actually say them. Allison figured Maria should know. In fact, from where Allison was in her motherhood journey—still in her nightgown at 10:00 some mornings—a mother of three who actually had some makeup on once in a while seemed like some sort of Solomon.

During the babbling stage, children love making sounds, putting consonants and vowels together for the sheer joy of it. However, once a child begins deliberate mimicking, his language becomes specific.

At this stage, the parent can help stimulate growth toward communication by repeating sounds back to the child. Again, this is a pattern most people fall into without any conscious effort; baby says, "babababababa," and Daddy or Mommy repeats it, pausing to see if the baby will say some more. He usually does. This give and take—pausing between vocalizations, then reflecting back what baby has said—is the child's first experience with conversational language.

During the mimicking stage, the child begins to also recognize the metrical patterns of his native tongue. In France, where the accent is usually on the last syllable, babies around six months of age begin to show a preference for such words. Their American counterparts, however, are more responsive to words with stressed first syllables, such as *mommy* and *daddy* and *baby* and *doggie*.

While the child is still doing a lot of exploring with sounds during the mimicking stage, he is also beginning to modulate and practice greater control.

Typical Order of Oral Sounds

b, d, p, m, n, t, and vowels

g, k, ng, w, h, j

f, v, th, sh, ch, s, z, r, l

Blends: tr, pl, br, st, sw

One of Tina's favorite spots was the pet store. Allison discovered this early on when she and a friend from Lamaze class had been wheeling strollers along the shops in town and ventured in to give their babies a closer look at the doggies in the window. Tina loved all the animals, especially the fish in the dramatically darkened room in the back. Since they still lived in an apartment and couldn't have pets, anytime Allison had a few extra minutes, she took Tina for a trip to the pet store. Once the owner began to recognize them, she stopped asking if they

needed help, and just nodded her head toward the back room when they came in. Sometimes she came in to chat, stooping down to Tina's level and pointing to the brightly colored fish. "See the fish?" she would ask. Maybe that's why she was so proud when Tina said her first real word in her store. Well, kind of. "Shish," said Tina clear as a bell. All three of them knew what she meant. "Yes, Tina—fish," the pet store owner said. Allison couldn't wait to get home and write about it in the baby book.

◆　◆　◆　◆

Baby's First Word

One of the highlights of baby's first year is his first word. Not a random *mama* or *dada* ("Did he really know he was calling me, honey?"), but one unmistakably connected to the specific person or object. Keep in mind that a child's first word may not be a true word. But if your pet terrier steps into the room and your baby squeals in delight and says, "Goggy!" then that is as good a word as they come.

Now the parent can reflect what the child has said with a slight variation, "Yes, doggie." Keep it short and simple, only two words: an acknowledgment and the correct pronun-cia-tion. Use encouragement—a conversational rather than cor-rective tone of voice. Your acceptance of his first words encourages the child and makes him eager to try more. This principle of reflecting without specifically correcting is the way to handle all language development through the early years.

Keep in mind that no matter how important, language is only one part of your child's total development. There is much going on in the first year. There are advances in gross

motor control, fine motor control, sensory perception—
many different areas. Try to stay relaxed and happy with
your child, not pushing unless for some reason your child
needs it (as in the case of Down syndrome).

Try not to compare your child with others, unless you see
specific red flags—significantly large delays in meeting developmental milestones (see appendix C). In these cases, you
want to obtain intervention services as quickly as possible.
But remember that you will always see a broad range of language development among children. Having opportunities
to be around a lot of children the same age as your own—in
play groups, while volunteering in the church nursery—can
help you keep things in perspective.

*Tina was a year old when Steve had a job transfer. It couldn't
have worked out better for their little family; now they would be
a hop, skip, and jump from Allison's parents. They had always
wanted Tina to be able to see them more often.*

*Steve and Allison fell in love with a little housing develop-
ment that seemed to have been laid out with young families in
mind. The main streets bent around little cul-de-sacs lined with
townhouses. Though the trees were newly planted and it would
take a while for the neighborhood to look completely comfortable, it already looked settled in. They especially found a lot of
charm in the cul-de-sac that would become their home.*

*"Toddler Row" the neighbors had dubbed it. Play equip-
ment dotted the front lawns and was shared by all the children
while the moms enjoyed discussing what they knew and what
they were learning about their children.*

As Tina learned to sit up and to crawl, she was part of the ever-growing group (some of the moms were having their second babies now). At Tina's age, Allison learned, babies don't interact much. They're just aware of each other, mostly doing their own things. Side-by-side play they call it.

Allison also noticed that what she had read was true; the girls seemed to be picking up words a little faster than the boys. But it was obvious among all the children that the second year was marked by a rapid accumulation of words.

By the end of the first year, most babies are saying a word or two in addition to calling Mommy and Daddy by name. But that's only one side of their language ability.

Every child really has two vocabularies, active and passive. The active vocabulary, sometimes called expressive language, consists of words the child is able to say, for instance, when she points to a tank in the pet store and says "fish." The passive vocabulary consists of words the child understands when others speak them, such as when Grandpa says, "Where is Timmy's nose?" and little Timmy points to his nose without speaking. When we say that a one-year-old's vocabulary is made up of two words, we're talking only of words she actually says, not of words she actually knows. Throughout the preschool years the child's passive vocabulary is much larger than his active one.

It may not occur naturally to parents to provide their child with a lot of words at this period of development—after all, what they see is a child working to say *mommy,*

<hr>

Creating a Language-Rich Environment for Infants

If you could raise your child's I.Q. through doses of some special elixir, you'd do it in a heartbeat—no matter how awful the taste. How blessed we are that getting our children off to a good start is such a sweet thing to accomplish.

Try these good old-fashioned methods:
- Lullabies
- Nursery rhymes—Jack and Jill, Humpty Dumpty, etc.
- Repetitive songs—"Old McDonald," "The Wheels on the Bus," etc.
- Finger plays
- Naming everything at home, at the zoo, at the beach, out the car window
- Picture books
- Puppets and stuffed animals "talking" to the child

<hr>

daddy, bye-bye, doggie, cat, and *fish.* But the creation of a language-rich environment is important even in the early years.

If you're a talker naturally, keeping up a "conversation" with your baby will come effortlessly. If not, you may need to make a conscious effort to learn to talk to your baby. Start by talking naturally, describing what your baby or you are doing:

"Shake, shake, shake the rattle!"
"Put it in the basket."

"Let's eat lunch."
"Up, up, up we go!"
"Where's the baby?"
"Up in the high chair."
"Put on your bib."
"Mommy's making cereal."

Use short sentences and a lot of inflection. While holding your gaze steady on baby, say a few words or ask a question, then pause to give the baby a chance to "talk" back to you. His response may be arm waving or grunting or cooing, but it's sure to show his excitement. This is the beginning of conversation, taking turns expressing feelings and listening.

Make it a practice to name everything in baby's sight— spoon, kitty, banana, cup. Long before he can speak, the child is storing up many words. The more words he comes in contact with, the more he'll have at his disposal when the time comes for him to explode into language.

Shortly after his first birthday, the child develops the physical control of his mouth and tongue necessary to produce words at will. Because he is now walking and climbing, he is learning more and more about things in his environment. You will notice imitative behavior, such as jabbering on the phone.

At age eighteen months or so, you will witness what is best described as a language explosion. After slow but steady progress, baby suddenly begins acquiring words at the mind-boggling rate of ten to twelve per day. As always, understanding outpaces vocalization. Most words will remain part of his passive vocabulary for a long time before they become part of his spoken language. Still, the richer the passive vocabulary, the better for the child.

◆ ◆ ◆ ◆

Allison and Steve were talkers themselves. They found it easy to include Tina in conversations, using smaller words and simpler sentences. They also enjoyed reading, then asking questions about the pictures on each page, like "Where is the cat?" "Where is his hat?" "Show me the window." "Is it raining outside?"

Tina also liked to watch Sesame Street and loved the characters. But Allison and Steve had decided early on to limit TV, sensing that it was a passive form of learning. Of course, sometimes they needed a break and let Tina watch a video, but they tried not to overdo it. Time spent reading or playing with Tina was more beneficial, they felt. Besides, they enjoyed it! She really seemed to be the brightest little girl they'd ever known—even if she was their daughter!

"Wuzzat?" Tina would ask, pointing to pictures in books. She loved new words, soaking them up like a sponge. When she put two words together for the first time, it was hard for Allison to be firm. "No nap," Tina announced. "Yes nap," Allison managed to answer with a straight face.

◆ ◆ ◆ ◆

Usually before the second birthday another amazing development takes place; you might be ready to leave the house but caught up in a last-minute search for keys when your little one grows impatient and demands, "Go now!" A developmental milestone has been reached—baby's first sentence. You acknowledge, "Yes, we are going now, but we need our keys." After all, maybe he knows where they are!

READING TIPS

Books are the best! Even if you never really connected with reading before, you may discover as a parent— through reading with your little one—that it's a lot of fun. One of the greatest benefits of having kids is the opportunity it gives us to grow and to change. The first step to putting your child on the path to a lifelong love of reading is to fall in love with reading yourself.

Actually, falling in love with reading isn't that hard to do. Take it from someone who's been reading to kids for twenty-seven years, children's books are fun to read—especially when you know what to look for.

Looking for the *right* books is important. There are a lot out there to choose from—and a lot to avoid. If you're going to take the time to cuddle up and read a book to your child (especially if your time is limited) why not spend it wisely?

What makes some books better than others? To start with, the best children's literature—like all good literature— presents a problem that needs resolution, as in *Caps for Sale*, in which the capseller must get his caps back from the rascally monkeys. In the end, the story shows how the problem is resolved and reestablishes feelings of security and well-being, as in *Good Dog, Carl*. Better yet, it teaches a lesson, very subtly, along the way, as in *Where's Our Mama?* which not only reminds children to stay in the same place when they are lost but also validates each listener's belief that her mama is the best.

Don't Tell Me, Show Me

Many entertaining and engaging stories carry an extra bonus; a theme that reinforces a value or virtue. The message in *The Rainbow Fish* may be clear to adults—pride isolates a person, and sharing feels good. Even though the theme is never stated directly, we can easily put it into words ourselves. The child's mind works differently. A statement of theme would mean nothing to him. Yet through the story of the rainbow fish's conflict and resolution, the unspoken theme can have a powerful impact on the character of the child.

Children, especially, think and perceive on a concrete level. During the preschool years they are incapable of abstract thinking. Teaching them about kindness, generosity, courage, etc., can only take place through stories.

Most of us—children and adults—would rather have someone *show* why something works than *tell* us why. Few of us enjoy being clobbered with ideas. We'd rather hear stories. Experts refer to the themes underlying plot lines as subliminal messages. For Christians, the Holy Spirit undoubtedly has a hand in shaping us through well-presented stories. That's why the parables of Jesus are such wonderful teaching devices.

Rhythm and Repetition

Two characteristics you will often find in children's books are rhythm and repetition. Both work to keep the child focused on the book. Skillful children's authors know this will keep a child coming back again and again. As you read, emphasize the rhythm and repetition in the text. Besides making a book more fun for you and your child, each also makes it easy for the child to memorize the text and "read" it on his own.

BUILDING A LIBRARY

Even if your baby is very young and not yet capable of understanding the words, you can still use the following guidelines when you select books for him, especially books you are buying to build a library.

Guidelines for Buying Books

With an unlimited budget for books, you could build a library of everything that's out there for kids. Thank goodness our budgets are limited. That way we are forced to look for the best!

When considering a book, ask the following questions:

- Is this book attractive to children?
- Is this book fun to read—over and over again?
- Does this book have staying power—a timeless theme or classic message?
- Does this book reinforce (or at least not challenge) the values I want for my family?
- Does this book invite parent-child interaction?
- Is the author of this book speaking to children and not to their parents?

If you can afford it, I heartily recommend building a home library. (See appendix E for discount sources.) When your children see you buying books, they realize that books have value and worth. There are many inexpensive paperback editions out with the same wonderful illustrations as the expensive hardbacks. For the cost of a video rental you can get a book or two to have around for many years.

Books are a worthy investment. Children treat books like old friends. They want to spend a lot of time with the ones they really enjoy. No child's book is ever read just once. Children return again and again to a favorite book without losing interest or outgrowing it. They pore over the pictures, discovering new details, thinking to themselves and talking to others about them.

Trust me, a good book will hold your child's attention much longer than most toys—and books have the advantage of not missing pieces or cluttering up your house as much. Books also have a longer lifespan than toys. Books have a way of growing up with a child. I've heard of college-bound teens who've asked their parents not to get rid of their childhood libraries—they want them for their own children.

Check secondhand stores and garage sales for used books. But do make sure they are in good repair before buying them. If you bring books with torn or drawn-on pages into your home, it will give your child the idea that mistreating books is okay. If you want your child to respect books, they must be in good condition.

Let grandparents, friends, and family know that you would love to receive books for baby gifts. If you have several children and they receive books for gifts, you will build a respectable library faster than you think.

Public libraries are a good resource for borrowing books (they also have sales of old books sometimes), and trips to the library have a lot of charm. But here you would be wise to give your child a lot of guidance. Many books have themes incompatible with the needs of children and perhaps with your own convictions. I always page through the books my children pick before actually checking them out. I have weeded out some real junk that way.

If your library has a story hour, check to see which book the librarian is reading before taking your child. Stories about witches, goblins, and ghosts for instance (standard fare during Halloween season) are never appropriate for toddlers, who are not yet capable of distinguishing between reality and fantasy.

Still, these are issues you will face later on. Books for babies are straightforward and innocent—pictures of familiar things or stories like *Goodnight Moon* that just sound irresistible.

In the beginning, you may want to start with board books. These are the more indestructible editions, with heavy unbendable pages. In between readings, I keep ours in a basket on the floor. You might want to do this also—so your own little one can choose them at playtime even when you're not there to supervise.

CUDDLE UP

From the time you can hold your baby in a sitting position, both of you can share the joy of reading together.

Reading before bedtime is a wonderful tradition to begin early on, but try not to limit reading to only one time. Try after lunch or after playtime too. In addition to spending quality time together, you will be planting some prereading skills that will help your child later on. Early read-alouds build good listening habits, laying the foundation for a child who can cooperate and concentrate and who will develop good comprehension skills.

So start early!

Holding your baby in your lap, place the book in front of the two of you at a comfortable level. Exaggerate the care with which you pick up just the corner of the page and turn it. If the text seems too complicated, use your own words— but remember—the child's ability to understand is always well beyond the words he can say. Your voice and inflection play an important part in his understanding. As you read the text, point, sliding your finger smoothly just under the words.

What is going on during this time? In addition to the warm closeness and the sharing of a story and possibly a message, you are also laying the groundwork for your child to respect books and treat them carefully. Through the left to right movement through the text, you are planting some subtle information: reading moves left-to-right across the page, one line follows another, and we read the left page before the right.

That so much valuable learning could be going on during such a pleasant interlude is like icing on the cake— and all the more reason to find those moments to read with your child.

BOOK RECOMMENDATIONS
Six Months to Two Years

If you are new parents and just beginning your adventure into the world of children's books, hold onto your hats!

There are years of fun ahead for you and your children!

After twenty-seven years of reading books to my own children as well as to students, I know which books deserve more than a casual read or two, which can please now and later, and which can even stand up to a few hundred readings (don't laugh until you've had a few children!).

With eleven children and two parents who love books, our family has built quite a children's library—close to two thousand volumes. They line a wall and a half in my office. Along with a cozy couch, they invite my children to read while Mama writes.

All this by way of saying, I didn't have to go very far to find books to recommend. To share the best and brightest in children's books with you, I've simply pulled out the best from my children's shelves.

The fact that some were pretty worn—having spent a lot of time in children's laps and hands—made them easier to spot on the shelves. I left behind their wallflower cousins and chose the ones whose dance cards were always full.

In my recommendations I listed the date of first publication so you would get a sense of the timelessness of some of these stories with true kid appeal. However, I checked carefully to make sure that each book I've recommended is currently in print and available. You will find them on the shelves, or by order through your local library or bookstore, or on the Internet at www.amazon.com.

These books have been a major part of my life for twenty-eight years. It is with great pleasure that I introduce these faithful family friends. As you get to know them, I am sure you will love them too.

Board Books

There are shopping cartfuls of board books available, but they seem to appear and disappear a little more quickly than other children's books. For this reason, I have recommended those that are my very favorites, ones that promise to be around for a while.

Also, each year, more and more children's classics—like *Goodnight Moon, Runaway Bunny, Corduroy,* or *Winnie the Pooh*—are being released in board book format. Browse through the children's section of your bookstore to see what's available this month. Buying a classic in board book form (as long as it isn't condensed) means your investment will add up to more years of reading.

All Aboard Noah's Ark (also *In the Beginning, Baby Moses, Jonah and the Whale, Little David and the Giant*), Mary Josephs, Random House, 1994

Small, pudgy books that fit well in small, pudgy hands, with little flaps to peek under on every page. Each tells a familiar Bible story in simple, childlike language.

The Baby Bible Story Book, Robin Currie, Chariot Victor, 1994

Bible stories scaled for the smallest, with lots of interactive opportunities (pretending to hammer while

Noah builds the ark, clapping hands as God closes the door behind the animals, wiggling fingers for the rain). Each draws a simple conclusion and offers a child's prayer. Cute illustrations.

Little Duck's Friends (also others in the series of Squeeze-and-Squeak Books), Muff Singer, Joshua Morris, 1994

Special pages cut around a soft plastic duck invite the child to press and make him squeak. The story line explains, in rhyme, how each animal has special gifts—as does baby!

Pat the Bunny, Dorothy Kunhardt, Golden Press, 1984

Lots of people give this book as a shower gift. An unabashedly old-fashioned and delightful book with lots of "fingers on" fun for tots. A must for all.

A Pocketful of Promises (also *Proverbs, Psalms*), Helen Haidle, Gold'n'Honey/Questar, 1994

I love these books! Each closes with a piece of Velcro and opens like a pocket. Inside, a sentence and charming illustration convey an important Bible truth. Example: "You are never alone. God is always with you" (based on Matthew 28:20). Good theology for parents too!

Where Does Little Puppy Go (My First Puzzle Books), Jim Becker, Cartwheel Books, 1992

A cardboard puppy puzzle piece, attached by a ribbon, can be taken for a walk or to chase butterflies through the pages of this book.

READ-ALOUD STORIES

While these books can captivate the attention of very young children, their appeal and value extend well beyond these early years. A four- or five-year-old will find much of interest in Richard Scarry's *Best Word Book Ever*, for example. Other books, such as *Caps for Sale* or *Noisy Nora*, will later double as your child's first readers.

Best Word Book Ever, Richard Scarry, Golden Press, 1963
     Every one of my children—from the oldest (now 27) to the current toddlers—has found plenty to hold his or her attention for hours in this terrific vocabulary builder, chock-full of pictures of almost everything a child could possibly learn to name.

Brown Bear, Brown Bear, What Do You See? Bill Martin, Jr., illustrated by Eric Carle, Holt and Company, 1967
     A story built on rhythm and repetition, highlighting colors and animals. Little ones love this first memory stretcher.

Caps for Sale, Esphyr Slobodkina, Scholastic, 1940
     Be dramatic! Shake your fists! Stomp your feet! You and your toddler will have so much fun with this wonderful story in which common sense prevails over temper tantrums!

Chicken Soup with Rice, Maurice Sendak, Scholastic, 1962
     Another R&R (rhythm and repetition). This one is filled with a feeling of humor. Impossible to read without a smile.

Good Dog, Carl, Alexandra Day, Simon & Schuster, 1985

A wonderful introduction to story sequence: plot, scenes, characters, emotion—will they get the house in order before Mother comes home?—all without a single word of text! Toddlers and parents can have a lot of fun with this engagingly illustrated tale.

Goodnight Moon, Margaret Wise Brown, Harper & Row, 1947

If you did a survey of children's favorite books by asking children themselves, this gem of a book would surely top the list. A bunny gets ready for sleep, saying good night to each special object he sees from his bed. A soft and soothing farewell at the end of any little one's busy day.

Jamberry, Bruce Degen, Harperfestival, 1985

An energetic romp through the colorful world of berries with a rollicking rhyme-spouting bear and a straw-hatted boy. There's so much to celebrate!

The Lost Sheep (first of a series including *The Rich Farmer* and *The Lost Coin*), Nick Butterworth, Multnomah, 1986

This parable, with a highly satisfying meaning for young ones gets a child-friendly treatment and irresistibly amusing illustrations. Really cute.

"More More More" Said the Baby, Vera B. Williams, William Morrow & Co., 1990

A trio of love stories: three toddlers enjoying tender moments with father, grandmother, and mother. Catchy toddler words, bright vivid pictures. Natural, wholesome, current, multicultural.

Noisy Nora, Rosemary Wells, Scholastic, 1973

Poor Nora! The lovable mousette experiences all the pangs of the child-in-the-middle, caught between the demands of baby brother and the bossiness of big sister. Catchy meter and playful illustrations make for a wonderfully satisfying mouse's tail—oops, I mean tale.

On Mother's Lap, Ann Herbert Scott, Scholastic, 1992

An Eskimo boy finds a lot of room on mother's lap for all his favorite things, but thinks there's none for baby sister. Mother shows him there's room for all. A wonderful remedy for new-baby blues.

Read-Aloud Bible Stories, volumes 1–4, Ella K. Lindvall, Moody, 1982–95

These large volumes with bold full-page illustrations on one side and simple text on the other have a lot of kid appeal. One unusual feature is that Jesus' face is never seen, thus avoiding some of the stereotypes and allowing room for the child's imagination. Bible stories are retold with rhythm, repetition, and loads of enthusiasm— when the apostles fish where Jesus tells them, "Big fish/ little fish/ wiggly fish/ Oh my!"

The Runaway Bunny, Margaret Wise Brown, Harper & Row, 1942

Another must-have from the author of *Goodnight Moon*. The story of "Everybunny" who, like every typical toddler, wants to assert his independence from Mother while being reminded she will always be there for him. Beautifully illustrated, a message with lasting value.

Shoes, Elizabeth Winthrop, Harper & Row, 1986

A rollicking, rhyming tribute to a toddler's most-loved item of apparel. Just for fun!

The Toddler's Bible, V. Gilbert Beers, Victor, 1992

Straight through the Bible, toddler-style. The author's ability to translate complex stories into a few simple sentences is sure to delight. Read this during the toddler years, and before you know it, your child will be reading it back to you.

The Very Hungry Caterpillar (also *The Very Busy Spider, The Grouchy Ladybug*, etc.), Eric Carle, Philomel Books, 1984

A children's library with no books by Eric Carle would be like a chocolate chip cookie with no chips. This author understands how to captivate even the most easily-distracted child. Read this one with lots of finger drama and chomping noises and your child is sure to be delighted.

Where's Our Mama? Diane Goode, Scholastic, 1991

Such a sweet story! Two children who have lost their mama have trouble finding her only because they see her as the best, the wisest, the most beautiful. The *gendarme* (French policeman) is astonished to find that she is just a mama like everyone else's. For fun, read it with your best French accent!

Chapter Two

SET

Two to Five Years

*B*y the time Tina was two, she was using a few two-word sentences: "Go bye-bye." "Daddy home."

One day Allison was doing laundry when she noticed the house seemed just a little too quiet. She'd been a mother long enough to know that signal meant something was up.

She found her daughter in the kitchen at the edge of a white puddle. "Uh-oh, Mommy, spill milk!" Tina said solemnly when she saw her mom. The puddle was spreading and the new kitty was lapping at the edges. Tina seemed fascinated by it all. Allison guessed that's why she hadn't cried. There was a bowl and a box of cereal on the counter; the milk container was lying on its side on the floor.

Allison felt her temper rising—she had so much to do this morning without cleaning up more messes! Then, making a quick decision to make the best of the situation (Allison couldn't claim to be perfect, but she always tried), she used the opportunity instead to teach Tina first how to clean up a spill, then how to pour without spilling.[2]

Only after the kitchen was back in order did Allison realize that Tina had actually put four words together. Wow! That was almost a sentence!

It was things like this that kept Allison going as a mom. Sometimes it seemed as though no one thought that what she did was very important at all. Her mother was encouraging, though. "I'm glad you're home with Tina, Allie," she said. "I feel like I missed a lot when you were growing up." Allie felt like she had missed a lot too; being a latchkey kid had been pretty lonely. Of course, being a stay-at-home mom could feel lonely too. But the wonder of watching her own child grow and change—having a hand in it all—made it worth it.

Watching Tina day by day gave Allison a powerful sense of the miraculous, at least when she slowed down enough to think about it. For each new milestone—no matter how effortless it seemed when Tina met it—Allison knew much had been going on beneath the surface.

"I mean, she really wants to do things for herself," she concluded when she told Steve about the spill that night at dinner. "Don't you think that's kind of neat? And she's talking so much—more and more each day."

Now We're Talkin'

At two the real language explosion begins, making the preceding months look more like warning temblors than the real thing. The child now has a wide range of two-word sentences—and two words can say a lot!

Two-Word Sentences Can:

- identify (See duck!)
- claim (my mommy)
- ask (where Daddy?)
- describe (good yogurt)

At two years of age, a child has approximately a 270-word vocabulary. This will increase almost four-fold in the next year.

Expressive Vocabulary

12 months:	3 words
15 months:	19 words
18 months:	22 words
21 months:	120 words
24 months:	270 words
3 years:	1000 words
5 years:	2000 words
Adult:	20,000–60,000 words

Don't forget: a child understands at least twice as many words as he speaks!

Keep in mind that these ages are approximate, that even twins raised together will exhibit differences in timetables.

Language development takes place while the child is also learning many other skills, including:

- gross motor
- fine motor
- self-reliance
- social

Factors in Language Development

- Sex (girls develop at a faster rate than boys)
- Birth order
- Intelligence
- Overall health
- Structure of the mouth
- Home environment

Of all the influences in language development, the only one over which parents have control is the atmosphere in the home. How a child's parents relate to him or her is all-important. In fact, it is more important than the parents' education level. Regardless of background, any parent who wants to give his or her child the best can commit to creating an environment rich in language opportunities.[3]

You can encourage your child's speech best by showing approval and carrying the conversational ball. Talk about everything. Look for the details around you. Point to the flowers, the clouds, the sights from the car. For those who need some ideas for putting a little more *oomph* in communicating with little ones, the following boxes give some suggestions.

Toddler Talk Tips

Rule Number One: Never correct a child's speech directly.

Rule Number Two: Use normal conversation to model the expanded form.

Add adjectives

Child: *My ball.*

Parent: *Yes, that is your big blue ball.*

Fill in the blanks

Child: *Cat out.*

Parent: *Yes, the cat is going outside.*

Refine verb tense

Child: *Duck swim.*

Parent: *Yes, the duck is swimming.*

Expand thought

Child: *Milk gone.*

Parent: *Yes, you drank all the milk and it is gone!*

Stretch sentences into paragraphs

Child: *Daddy byebye.*

Parent: *Yes, Daddy is gone to work. He went in his car. He will be back at dinnertime.*

Ask questions

Parent: *What will you do when Daddy comes home?*

While working to enrich your child's conversation, continue expanding his vocabulary, providing words for everything in sight. As often as possible, take your child with you shopping. Go to the zoo, the country, the city. Look through magazines and catalogs together. Give him as many names for things as you can.

Give Clear Commands

Efforts to expand sentences are best when they sharpen focus rather than add confusion. Keep commands short and direct.

Not: *"I want you to take care of putting the toys where they belong."*
But: *"Please pick up these toys."*

Can you hear the difference? Then your child will also.

Remember, a child's expressive language is only a portion of the words he has stored in his memory—and during the toddler years his mind is like a sponge, soaking up everything it touches. Just as God gave Adam mastery over the animals by giving him the responsibility of naming them, your child's ability to name things makes him feel confident of his place in the world.

Still, God created language for more important reasons than stewardship. He also gave us language to enable us to build strong relationships—with each other and with him. From the earliest years, a child needs to learn to be comfortable with the language of feelings, use words to express emotions, seek comfort, and cope with problems.

"Are you upset because Tommy doesn't want to share his truck? Maybe we should give him more time."

"Are you worried about the new Sunday school class? Everybody worries the first time. I'll make sure the teachers know who you are before I leave."

"Are you afraid when the lights are off at night? Did you know God is always with you? Let's pray about it."

Words, Words, Words

Your child's curiosity level will never be higher than during the toddler years. Language opportunities are all around.

- Colors
- Numbers
- Community helpers
- Feelings
- Parts of the body

- Vehicles
- Rhyming words
- Movement words (jump, hop)
- Relational words (in, under)
- Opposites (off, on)

During this time of intense language acquisition, parents do well to drop all baby talk and consistently model correct speech. Using complete sentences calls the child up to the next level.

Instead of: "Daddy go byebye."
Try: "Daddy's going byebye."
Or better: "Daddy's going to work."

My oldest son, Joshua, had some interesting pronunciations of words as a toddler. He said "pan-a-cake" instead of pancake, "hamgurber" instead of hamburger, and "theetyer" instead of theater. His big sisters, as well as his parents, found this so amusing that we never corrected him. In fact, we enjoyed his new words so much we started using them at home ourselves. Only when he got into an argument with younger brother Matthew about a word—Joshua was insisting that it was *panacake* rather than *pancake*—did we realize we had carried on the joke a little too long.

Little One's Logic 101

Begin early to build your child's reasoning skills. Show how language is used to cope with the unexpected: "Since it's raining, we can't go out today like we planned. That's disappointing, isn't it? What could we do instead? Maybe we could invite Grandma over." In this simple way, a mom has:

- acknowledged a problem
- acknowledged her child's feelings
- shown that they can take charge of the situation so as to not feel like victims
- offered an attractive alternative

Use clear pronunciation and a pleasant tone of voice. Remember, you are modeling how you want your child to talk to others. Though we have a TV and satellite dish, I do not allow my children to watch sitcoms on major networks, because the tone of voice the characters use is usually sarcastic, argumentative, whiny, or disrespectful. Children sound like what they're used to listening to. Children are little mirrors. Down to the smallest details, they are reflections of us. If you say *sumthin'* instead of *something*, your child probably will also.

> ## Help Him Have a Head Start in Speech
>
> You are the first speech teacher your child has—so try to be the best!
>
> - Pronounce clearly but comfortably
> - Keep the volume down
> - Speak at a comfortable pace—not too fast or too slow
> - Use a pleasant tone of voice
> - Choose interesting vocabulary, but not more than one step above your child's level

With ten children still at home—not one of them quiet or reserved—and especially every Sunday afternoon with Samantha and Kip (our oldest daughter and her husband) and my three grandsons over for dinner, you can imagine the decibel level at our house. It's like a party where the noise level keeps rising as each person tries to talk over the background conversations. When our dinner table starts getting a little too loud for my taste, I just start whispering. Since I would like my children to be a little more soft-spoken, I try (with the emphasis of course on the *try*) to keep my own voice down.

Always remember to use the most subtle and indirect form to correct your child's immature speech—modeling the right way yourself, very casually and conversationally.

"See fishy over dere."
"Yes, I see the fish over there."
"Pitty cat."
"Yes, that is a pretty cat."

Don't try to force your child to say things correctly. Sometimes he can't. Some consonant sounds and combinations are actually very sophisticated and appear rather late developmentally.

So much is going on! Even as your child is acquiring vocabulary at an astonishing rate, even as he continues to perfect his pronunciation, he is also absorbing the syntax of our English language. Syntax is the way our language is organized to convey information; these are the rules that enable us to communicate with understanding.

Here is another dimension of human speech that leaves the "experts" with as many questions as answers. Since each language has different syntax (rules governing sentence arrangement, plurals, word tenses, etc.), linguists can say only that we are born with the capacity to absorb the syntax of our native tongue. But they don't know how it happens.

Again, I see God's hand clearly.

And you will too as you watch your child absorbing the surprises and subtleties of the English language. You won't need to sit down and give your child formal lessons in grammar. Simply by listening, he will pick up the rules.

As he learns the rules, he will adhere to them rigidly. What will you think when he runs in to tell you:

"Mommy, the cat bringed in two mouses!"

Maybe you'll recognize that this represents a great deal of sophistication for your child. He has learned:

- that verbs have tenses (adding -ed means it already happened)
- that nouns have plurals (adding s shows there is more than one of something)

No small accomplishment! And all without a single direct lesson from you.

Now your job is not to correct him, but to take him further into the subtleties I mentioned simply by modeling. Ideally, your child should never even notice what you have done when you reflect his comments back to him:

"Oh, honey, let's go see. The cat brought in two mice?"

Practicing this type of correction will keep your child comfortable as he's learning to communicate. Remember, he *wants* to do well. Children have feelings as real as ours. They also feel embarrassed when they make mistakes, less sure of themselves later. Give your child the best start by keeping communication encouraging and positive.

Listening Skills

Don't forget to help your child develop good listening skills too!

- Teach her to look directly at the person who is speaking.
- Whisper in her ear, then ask her to repeat what you have said.
- Ask questions about stories you have read.
- Most important of all—listen to her!

Keep in mind that one child's language development may appear to take place as a smooth progression from words to short phrases to sentences. Another child may travel a different learning curve, with spurts of rapid development followed by plateaus, or even some regression.

Remember, boys are generally six months or so behind girls in language development during the preschool years.

In addition, a child may experience upheavals that will set back or slow down his development for a while—the birth of a sibling, a family move, a grandparent's death. Try to accept your child's individual development pattern. Don't compare him to other children. And try not to pressure him in the area of language.

If at any time your preschool child begins to stutter, do both yourself and him a favor, don't take it seriously. A child's mind goes through periods where it races along faster than his organs of speech. One of my sons, now nine, has gone through four or five bouts of stuttering. I think it's because he is a near-genius and his brain has always been in higher gear than his mouth. When the stutter appears, we just become more patient—and we have instructed his brothers and sisters to do the same. He can take as long as he wants to say what he needs to say. He doesn't need our help.

Stuttering can disappear suddenly or gradually. But it usually disappears—provided parents have not made an issue of it. (See appendix F.)

Most importantly, enjoy! Accept and appreciate where your child is in his language development. Don't push; just invite him along on the journey to better speech through modeling and expanding. *Keep his early language based on love and good feelings,* just as it was in infancy.

Remember, reading is simply putting together symbols to produce the words you've usually heard spoken. Give your child the warmest and richest early language experience you can and he will bring those positive feelings with him to the written word as well.

Frustration Factors

Anyone who ever suffered at the hands of an overly-demanding foreign language teacher (like my own first French teacher, may God rest her hard-to-please soul) can sympathize with how kids feel when they experience the following:

- high expectations
- pushing
- over-correcting
- teasing, poking fun

Avoid these little spoilers. Use the Golden Rule with your children and you will never go wrong.

Tina was making such great progress, it seemed silly to worry. Yet Allison did. She wondered whether what she was doing was adequate to meet her daughter's needs. Some of Tina's playmates were away now during the day—their moms had gone back to work. A couple of them had found good day-care situations, and the children seemed to be doing pretty well.

Even some of the stay-at-home mothers Allison knew were starting to put their children in preschool. Most said they wanted to give them a head start before kindergarten.

Allison wasn't sure what she should do. Were there certain things Tina should be learning? She didn't really want to send her daughter off to school already. Besides they couldn't really afford it. Was there something she could do at home with Tina?

At church there was a group of moms who home schooled their children, but Allison found it hard to approach them for advice. They seemed so locked in to the home schooling thing. She sensed that they were looking for some kind of commitment she didn't feel ready to make. She really didn't know if she wanted to home school or not. And after all, she had a few more years to make that decision.

Still she worried. Newspapers and magazines were sounding the alarm that schools were failing to teach basic reading skills. The President had even mentioned it as part of his reelection campaign. But his goal of everyone reading by the third grade sounded more like an admission of defeat than a higher challenge.

Then there was the constant barrage of radio and TV ads for phonics programs. Allison never remembered hearing things like that when she was little. It seemed a whole industry had grown up overnight to help parents teach their children to read—a job they used to count on the schools to do. Evidently the schools couldn't do it.

Allison knew one thing: she didn't want Tina to be behind when she started school—wherever that might be. She knew of children who were learning the alphabet, maybe even reading, in preschool. What could she do to help Tina?

Then again, was it too early for her to even be thinking about it?

◆　　◆　　◆　　◆

Reading: Time to Begin

When is the best time to start thinking about how your child will learn to read? Now!

Who is the best teacher? You.

You've already gotten some idea how important and qualified a teacher you are. After all, God entrusted you to pass on his gift of language to your child. If your heart's desire is to continue the natural progression of spoken language into writing and reading, he will give you the confidence you need to do it.

Never forget, you are your child's number one role model. She wants so much to be like you. If she sees you reading, if you have had cozy times reading together, she will naturally want to learn to read herself. Why wait to let someone else fulfill that wish?

It's a wonderful feeling to listen to a child read whom you have taught yourself, especially when that child is your own. How awesome it is to know he will be able to enjoy reading for years to come—perhaps eventually to your grandchildren.

I know this feeling from experience. And I also know it's not as difficult to accomplish as most people think.

The next half of this chapter will give you all you need to teach your children the skills they need to begin a lifelong love of reading. I can't stress enough the fact that you are already your child's primary teacher. Teaching reading is like the icing on the cake.

In the following pages you will learn how to:

- discover keys to unlock your child's reading potential;
- be liberated from the "teaching mystique" that convinces us that people need a credential to teach children a basic skill they themselves have used daily for decades;
- learn a few simple exercises that at the very least will develop your child's prereading skills to give him a head start in school; and
- be inspired to carry it all the way through.

Be confident of this: With a little consistency and faithful effort, you can teach your child to read before he goes to school—or at least give him the head start that will make the critical difference later between success and failure.

Why Start Early?

In our country, we are accustomed to thinking of children learning to read in first grade, or perhaps kindergarten. If you have always assumed that six is the appropriate age to begin reading, you may wonder why it would be wise to begin earlier.

Remember our earlier discussion of sensitive developmental periods? There are certain ages when the window of opportunity is widest for releasing the child's potential abilities. The sensitive period for learning reading skills is usually between the ages of four and five.

The word *usually* is important, because there is a wide range of variation among children in every phase of their development. Having been a mother of toddlers for twenty-seven years, as well as a preschool teacher, I know that very well. You can't push a child to do something he is not developmentally ready to do.

However, the more you understand how to meet the needs of the sensitive period and the wider you try to open that window, the more likely you are to see a smooth transition as the potential is released.

Practically speaking, this means that if you have three children and you put the simple *Ready, Set, Read!* ideas into practice, as each child reaches school age you may see three outcomes:

1. One five-year-old reads fluently.
2. One is reading-ready, with full command of phonetic sounds, ready to combine them into words.
3. One, even after a lot of practice, is still just beginning to know her sounds.

Does this mean that even though you put the same amount of effort into each of your children, you succeeded with only one? Not at all! It just means that they were all on different timetables.

Does this mean that your time has been wasted on the ones who will finish learning to read in school? Absolutely not!

In fact, your efforts may have been best spent on the one child who came nowhere near to reading. Let me explain. The child who learned to read easily would probably have learned to read easily at school. The child who entered school on the brink of reading will probably finish learning to read with little effort. But the third child, the one who learned only a few phonetic sounds—and perhaps with a great deal of effort on your part—will enter school in much better shape than with no previous exposure to letters and sounds.

We teach reading "early" because most children can learn easily and enjoy reading right away, but also because it is best for the few children who might otherwise later be labeled as having learning difficulties.

Reading specialist Toni S. Gould explains it best:

> For the past thirty-five years I have tutored four- and five-year-old children who have been diagnosed as having learning disabilities. Those children needed a great deal *more* help with learning sound-letter correspondence than allowed for in kindergarten or first grade. At the preschool level they had the free time to learn and to develop an interest in learning. Without exception, they experienced success in learning to read.
>
> In contrast, children with identical learning problems who were referred to me *after* they experienced failure had a harder time learning because of the initial blow to their self-esteem. Tragically, they need not have failed and would not have failed if [they had been] taught reading-readiness skills, especially sound-letter knowledge.[4]

The Sound Game and the Letter Game, which I will share later in this chapter, will give your child a foundation of early success. If you enjoy them and do them on a regular basis, you will probably have a reader on your hands.

But even if you do them on a less consistent basis, or even if your child is—like my own daughter Sophia—on a different developmental timetable, your time will be well spent. Even a child who can recognize only ten phonetic sounds and six letters will enter school with a head start.

What Becomes of Early Readers?

What of the child who knows how to read before kinder-garten? Won't he be bored? you may be wondering—and with good reason. After all, if it would be detrimental to your child's later academic success, you wouldn't want to spend the time teaching him too early.

It is safe to say that early reading is never harmful. For home schoolers, it poses no problem at all. And perhaps, if after reading this book you are successful in releasing your child's potential for reading, you will decide to go on to teach him other things as well. Home schooling is an easier decision to make when you realize it's one you only need to make a year at a time for each individual child.[5]

But even if your child goes to school reading well above second-grade level, his reading ability will not detract from his experience. A good teacher will find outlets for his reading ability, perhaps in reading aloud to the class or help-ing other children. In this case, be careful not to encourage your child to feel superior to other children, but to think of his early ability as a way to serve.[6]

If your child is an early reader, rejoice! Many early read-ers show throughout their education a more positive atti-tude toward learning. Because their first major academic task took place easily, they do not think of learning as a struggle. They are inquisitive and independent. All doors remain open to them.

The Spiritual Side of Reading

We start teaching the spiritual side by understanding reading in a different light, not as some invention of man, but as a gift God has given us. It follows naturally from his gift of spoken language. We can rely on the fact that when God has given us a gift, he will also help us unwrap it.

Reading is a potential built into each of us just as surely as our potential for spoken language. It is waiting to be released.

Just as the potential for spoken language needs certain environmental factors to be released, so does written language. Teaching reading is not the intimidating, specialized enterprise our culture has made it out to be. It is not pouring knowledge into a child's brain from without. Just as God has predisposed us to share oral communication, he has given us the inner workings we need to share written communication. The ability to read is part of the makeup of your child. Once you understand how it unfolds, you will see that teaching a child to read can be *almost* as easy as watching them learn to speak. Exceptions occur, however. In my own case, these were very beneficial.

My eighth child, Jonathan, who is five as I write this book, was born with Down syndrome.[7] I know God had a plan when he gave me Jonathan. But though I knew he would use this special son to teach me, I had no idea how much more I needed to learn. After twenty-two years with toddlers, I thought I was somewhat of an expert. Raising Jonathan has given me much greater perspective.

Children with Down syndrome have most of the same potentials as children with forty-six chromosomes, but they take longer and often need more intervention to be released. Like watching a movie in slow motion, parents with differently-abled children[8] find themselves in a situation where extra attention is focused on each developmental milestone. Instead of asking, "When will she take her first step?" we must ask, "How does the first step happen and what do I need to learn to help her get there?"

In the area of language, with Jonathan and now with the two baby boys with Down syndrome we've adopted since our ninth child Madeleine was born, our family wasn't able to watch the natural progression from cooing to babbling to first words. Instead, we had to initiate and press Jonathan toward the goals. Because their palates and tongues are shaped differently, because of low muscle tone, and because of slower cognitive skills, speech is just more difficult.

Still, children with Down syndrome nowadays learn to speak and to read. Spending more time and effort at each developmental level with Jonathan has given me greater understanding of how each of us is put together.

As I said, children like Jonathan are the exception, not the rule. So are children like the ones I taught in the seventies in Washington, D.C. As a Montessori teacher in a Head Start-funded inner-city preschool, I had some three-year-olds who entered my class with few—or in some cases, no—spoken language skills. These children did not suffer from mental handicaps like Jonathan. They suffered instead from economic and cultural deprivation—living conditions in which they were not surrounded by what they needed to have their gift of speech released. A year in a Montessori classroom with teachers and other less disadvantaged children made a remarkable difference in these children's abilities. Surrounded by the essentials they had been missing at home—mostly just hearing people speak and labeling things like colors and shapes—these children were speaking at levels within the normal range by the end of the year, though noticeably less well than the children whose potential for speech had been released at the appropriate time.

The help these children received through their hours in school, though delayed, was critical for their futures. There is a direct relationship between language and intelligence. As the ability to use language increases, so do cognitive growth and achievement.

The surest way to have an impact on your child's intelligence is to surround him with language and reading.

THE ROAD TO READING

Even if he's barely walking, you've already started your child on the road to reading. Each day you've taught him words and connected those words to the world around him. You've traveled miles of pages reading books together. (Nothing instills a love of literature like night after night of *Goodnight Moon* or *Curious George* on a cuddly lap.)

My friend Laura has an eight-year-old who runs through books like a locomotive down a track. Laura loves to tell of finding him as a toddler curled up under her covers, intently "reading" a thick bestseller. "I guess he'd seen me like that so often, it didn't even matter that there were no pictures. He just wanted to be like Mommy."

If a child has been exposed to books, and especially if he's grown up with adults who enjoy reading, he will need little coaxing to learn how to read.

What he will need are the tools.

During my training as a Montessori teacher, I was trained to provide a set of tools that will enable most children to read easily by the age of five or six. My years of classroom experience, with children from all economic and ethnic backgrounds, have confirmed that these techniques work. I have used this method at home, in the most casual and comfortable setting possible, to teach all but the youngest of my eleven children to read.

You, too, can teach your child to read. Or you can have fun with a few games and techniques that fit easily into your daily routine. No matter how much or how little you do, these early tools will pave the way for your child's later reading skills.

If you are still changing diapers, you might not have thought past potty training. But if your child has developed a vocabulary of fifty or more words, in diapers or out, he is ready.

THE SOUND GAME

The first goal is to make your child aware that words are composed of individual sounds. The Sound Game is guaranteed to get you there. You don't need any special equipment for the Sound Game. Play it in two to ten minute snatches anywhere—in the car or doctor's waiting room, while folding the clothes or loading the dishwasher.

The only preparation needed is to brush up on *phonetic sounds*. Remember to use these sounds rather than the names of letters.

Practice on your own first, isolating each letter. Try to clip the sounds, for instance *p* sounds like a puff of air, not like *puh*.

A Phonetic Alphabet — The Ear's the Thing

a -	as in apple	o -	ostrich
b -	bed	p -	peanut
c -	cat	q -	teach later, as qu (kw)
d -	daddy		
e -	Eskimo	r -	rabbit
f -	fan	s -	sing
g -	gate	t -	top
h -	hat	u -	up
i -	igloo	v -	victor
j -	jar	w -	wedding
k -	king (same as c)	x -	sounds like ks, as in box
l -	lemon		
m -	mommy	y -	yellow
n -	nest	z -	zebra

For the most part, the consonants are very obvious. But be careful with the vowels. Keep them crisp and clear.

What you will be doing is teaching your child—revealing to him, really—that words are made up of individual sounds. Although some letters have more than one sound, for now we use only the most common sound for the consonants and the short sound for the vowels—that is, the sound the vowel most often makes in three-letter words.

When you start, choose familiar sounds, those your child hears frequently in the words she uses. Because they have more emotional appeal and will therefore hold her attention, words about food and people she loves will have more learning impact.

Here's how your first session might go:

Mom: Let's think of some words that have *mmm* in them, like *m*ilk . . . *m*ommy . . . *m*oon.
Little Sweetie: Daddy?
Mom: I don't hear an *mmm* in daddy. *Mmm* . . . *m*arshmallow . . . *m*erry-go-round.
LS: Doggy?
Mom: *m*uffin . . . *m*ore . . . *m*aybe
LS: Cookie?
Mom: I don't hear an *mmm* in cookie. Cookie [say it emphasizing the sounds]. *C* . . . ookie . . . let's think of some words that have *c* [phonetic sound] in them, like *c*ookie . . . *c*ake . . . *c*at.
LS: Mommy?
Mom: *C*ar . . . *c*amel . . . *c*areful.

More likely than not, the first few times you will play this game solo. Your child may offer some words, but they probably will not be the ones you are looking for.

That's okay. Do not correct your child or tell him he is wrong in a direct way. Instead, just keep steering him toward the sound, giving as many examples as you can of words that mean a lot to him, as in the example above. Don't forget to use names of family members as well.

In the beginning, you are introducing an idea; that words are made up of individual sounds. As time goes on, your child will start to hear this as you keep training his ear to hear the different sounds. Then you can use the Sound Game to build vocabulary by using less familiar words.

This game can be played anywhere, at any time, and for any length of time. It can be interrupted by a phone call or to change the baby's diaper. You don't need to keep a record of any kind.

Keep playing often, and eventually—probably when you least expect it—your child will produce a correct response. Give him a great big hug!

From that point on you will be playing the Sound Game with a full-fledged partner. He will offer his own words. Now, since we asked for words that have the sound in them, if your child produces a word that does not begin with the sound but does contain it, say the word slowly, emphasizing the sound.

Also, since *c* and *k* sometimes have the same phonetic sound, if you ask for words with hard *c* and he offers king, then that is right. At this point your child does not know anything about letters. Likewise for *s* and soft *c*. Do not correct him as long as the *sound* is right.

> ## More Fun with Sounds
>
> - Play I Spy: "I spy something that starts with r."
> - Make a collage of cutout magazine pictures starting with the same sound.
> - Make a small booklet for each sound with one picture per page.
> - Sort pictures into sounds: all s words here, all m words there, etc.

If, after initially catching on, your child makes a mistake now and then, avoid responding by saying *no* and *wrong*. Simply steer him in the right direction, as follows:

"Do you hear a *p* in tiger? *T . . . i . . . g . . . r?* [Shake head.] You don't hear it? Do you hear a *p* in *p*o*p*corn?"

Children like the Sound Game. Just as a child enjoys pulling apart the petals of a flower to see how it is put together, once his attention is drawn to the fact that his language is made up of sounds, he will become interested enough to explore on his own.

Eventually, you may find your child playing on his own. Once you are sure he grasps the concept of individual sounds and can hear them clearly—even if you have not gone over every sound in the alphabet—he is ready for the Letter Game.

SESAME STREET

From its earliest days I have been very fond of *Sesame Street.* I saw the premier more than twenty years ago when my oldest daughter, Samantha, was eighteen months old. I remember how thrilled both of us were that she now had a show just for her, a show that would teach her in a uniquely fun-filled format. I was a stay-at-home mother then, living in Alexandria, Virginia, in a place much like Steve and Allison's "Toddler Row." The show provided a break for me to cook dinner, but I often found myself standing at the kitchen door, mesmerized by the action on *Sesame Street*.

For twenty-six years *Sesame Street* has delivered little disappointment. By exemplifying everyday harmony among races, the show has made a tremendous contribution to children's understanding and acceptance of cultural differences. *Sesame Street* was one of the very first television shows to incorporate children and adults with disabilities, including a regular who is deaf and uses sign language. I still get a thrill every time I see the little girl with Down syndrome. (Jonathan is madly in love with her). But even on the more subtle level of working out difficulties caused by those whose personalities clash (like Oscar and just about anyone) or who seem too slow (Mr. Snuffalupagus) or too air-headed (Big Bird), *Sesame Street* excels in championing kindness and tolerance.

The shows are always lively and unpredictable, full of tantalizing tidbits of information, such as what happens to garbage and how peanut butter is made. They teach urban children what life is like on a farm, and farm children what life is like in the city.

The characters are colorful and well textured (blue and clumpy, yellow and feathery) and absolutely full of human foibles and charm. Almost everyone has a personal favorite. In fact, I've often wondered if someone could devise a personality test from who your favorite *Sesame Street* character is.

Most people reading this book—young parents, like my daughter Samantha and some of my dearest friends[9]—grew up on *Sesame Street* themselves.

One of the teaching techniques *Sesame Street* popularized was sound-bite education. If you grew up on it, you know what I mean. Present a compelling image for a brief time, make it memorable, then move on. What a fun way to learn! And though the downside may be a shorter attention span, the show was enormously successful in imparting information to children—particularly in teaching children their alphabet.

But, oh, how I wish they had taught those letters differently!

Letter Sounds vs. Letter Names

Would it surprise you to know that the child who knows all twenty-six letters by name is really no closer to reading than the one who knows none at all? If so, then read on. Once you've seen how the phonetic approach to reading works, you'll understand completely. You'll see why—despite my admiration for *Sesame Street*—if I had my "druthers" I'd rewrite the way they teach the alphabet.

Knowing the names of letters does not facilitate reading at all; it may even make it more difficult. A child can look at a word and say, "dee - oh - gee" from breakfast to dinner and never have a clue that those letters spell the word *dog*. However, if he has learned the phonetic sounds for the letters rather than their names, he will string the sounds together easily to form a word with which he is familiar. What a joyful discovery! How easy it makes his journey into the world of reading.

That's why practice with phonetic sounds must come before the child even sees the letters that represent them.

Many methods of teaching reading bypass this important step. They do not follow the natural learning patterns of preschoolers (which may explain why, as I pointed out earlier, some educators don't understand that it is actually appropriate to teach reading to preschoolers). Often, when adults set out to teach children to read, they do so in a way that would be best for teaching another adult.

Children learn differently from adults. Their minds are not yet developmentally equipped to handle abstract concepts; they are still trying to find their footing in the concrete. In other words, you can tell them from now until the cows come home what a cow looks like, but until they see a cow they will not really be able to "see" it in their minds.

Likewise, giving children the *names* of letters, along with the symbols, gives them no solid foundation of what those letters really are, what they stand for, or what they mean. They remain merely empty symbols.

In the *Ready, Set, Read!* approach (patterned after Montessori), much time is spent pouring the foundation for reading. It is simple, inexpensive, and exceedingly easy to do. So easy, in fact, that you may not realize that as you have been playing the Sound Game with your child, you have already done it!

The true foundation for reading is in *sound* recognition. Through the Sound Game, the child comes to realize that our language is not only composed of words, but that each word is composed of individual sounds. His ear becomes trained to hear those sounds, alone and in many different combinations and patterns.

This is a concrete skill, a reality that the child needs to be on friendly terms with before she ever comes in contact with letters. Having given your child the experience of hearing all the sounds that make up the words she uses, you can now give her the symbol. Only now it will be more than an abstract symbol because she will know what it means. Once a child is familiar with the concrete, she has something to which she can attach the abstract symbol, like a ribbon that keeps the balloon from flying away.

The Letter Game

Once you have become a pro at the Sound Game—learning all the sounds, isolating them for your child and making him aware that they are parts of words—you have already become a qualified teacher of phonetics. You have laid all the groundwork necessary for the next step: introducing your child to the letters that serve as symbols for those sounds.

Letters to Touch and Teach

The only equipment you will need to play the Letter Game with your child is a set of lowercase letters.

Do not use uppercase letters at this point with your child. Think about it. Look at the book you have in your hands. How many letters are on this page? And how many are capitals? Not too many.

Capitals come into play only when the child begins to read books and construct sentences himself, and by then he'll be so secure in his reading that he will simply absorb them as he goes along. At this beginning stage, however, capitals are a distraction from the real work at hand. Knowing them will not help your child read.

Find a set of lowercase letters large enough for your child to trace with his fingers. Classic Montessori methods use sandpaper letters on coated particle board, which are beautiful but expensive. Fortunately, these are easily replicable with sandpaper, scissors, rubber cement, and heavy cardboard (see appendix G for instructions as well as sources for good, not-too-expensive alternatives).

Though sandpaper letters are not essential to the *Ready, Set, Read!* approach, they are well worth making (especially if you have, or plan to have, more children) because they are quite effective for teaching our little concrete thinkers. As you will see, we will not just be showing the letter to the child and giving its phonetic sound; we will be asking him to trace it and say it at the same time—practicing for future writing skills. Studies have shown that the more senses that are engaged in any learning process, the more efficient the learning and the longer the retention. That's why adults use audio-visuals instead of just telling, and why we take notes instead of just listening.

This is even more true with children. The more senses involved with learning letter-sound correspondence, the more readily children absorb the knowledge. The sandpaper letters have the distinct advantage of offering a textured surface for little fingers to trace, thereby not only engaging sight and hearing but also giving some very tactile feedback.

But if you don't have the time or budget, you're in a hurry, or you just want to keep things simple, go to your local toy store and buy a set of magnetic letters—lowercase only, remember—and stick them on the refrigerator door. Let your child play with them.

Correct Letter Formation

While you are on the path to reading, you will also be preparing your child for writing. Another benefit of the multisensory approach is that you will not only be teaching your child to recognize the letters visually but also to trace their shapes with his fingers. Get him off to the best start possible. If you need to, brush up on correct letter formation in appendix H.

Letters in Groups of Three

Teach your child letters in groups of three. Three will provide more interest than one or two, but will not be too overwhelming for your child to learn at one time. The groups are selected with the following factors in mind:

- contrast in phonetic sound
- contrast in appearance of letter
- usability in phonetic word formation (a phonetic word is one in which every letter says its true phonetic sound)

The first two contrasts will make it easier for your child to learn the letters. If you were trying to teach *f* and *v* in the same lesson (similar phonetic sounds) or *j* and *i* (similar appearance) your child would have more room for confusion.

Make it easier for your child to learn by maximizing the contrast between the shapes and sounds.

The third factor, useability in word formation, though not as critical to the child's success, will simply help your child be off and running sooner. As you will see, even before he knows all the letters, you will be encouraging him in the Word Game to make words of the letters he knows. So make sure the letters you choose to teach will go a long way, and introduce vowels early.

Suggested Sequence For Teaching Letters

For teaching letters, three-letter groups are optimum. Here is the order I have used for years;

m, a, t
s, i, p
c, r, j
n, o, g
f, u, d
b, e, w
v, l, x
h, y, z

Once you have taught your child the first three or four groups, he will be absorbing new letters easily in the Word Game, so the remaining letters will no longer *have* to be taught in any particular order.

(Note: The letters *k* and *q* are taught later, *k* as an alternative to the *c* sound and *q* after the child is learning phonetically.)

Teaching Technique

Maria Montessori devised the Three Period Lesson to teach letters, numbers, shapes, colors, or any kind of vocabulary to children in a way that maximizes their chances of success. It is a highly effective technique for any parent who would like to extend a child's vocabulary through the use of vocabulary cards.[10]

Three Period Lesson

First Period: Naming
The teacher presents and names three objects, one after another.

Second Period: Practice
The teacher provides the name, and the child chooses the matching object.

Third Period: Testing
The teacher asks the child to name the object.

The Three Period Lesson is also perfect for teaching sounds and letters. Just keep in mind that the first two periods require the greatest amount of time. Don't go to the third period until you're sure the child knows.

First Period: *Naming or identifying the letter sound*

Sit to the left of your child with the three letters face down (or if using something like magnetic letters, under a napkin).

Play the Sound Game briefly: "Let's think of some words with *m* in them . . . *m*ommy . . . *m*ister . . . *m*ountain." This is familiar territory. You have prepared your child, and at this point he knows what the game is about. After he contributes a few words, ask your child, with some drama,

"Do you want to see what *m* looks like?"

This is the key question and the key moment. Your child has the concrete knowledge of the letter through its sound. Now for the first time you are telling him that the letter is also something visual. What child wouldn't say yes?

Place the letter, almost with an attitude of reverence, on the table or the floor in front of you. You should both be seeing the letter right side up and you should be on your child's left. Even if you are left-handed—unless you suspect your child is also—always teach letters from this right-handed position.

What about Lefties?

The days when adults forced children into right-handedness are long gone. Most children show a clear preference for right-handedness, but others tend to show early ambidexterity, the ability to use both hands equally. In this case, since being left-handed does impose a little extra difficulty, we do offer objects to children from a position that encourages them to develop right-handedness—unless the child himself has shown a clear preference for the left.

If you do have a leftie, you will need to rethink everything you do with your child to make it work for him. (See appendix I.)

If you are using sandpaper letters or something similar, place the letter you are teaching on the table and turn it at an angle as you would a piece of paper you were about to write on. The bottom left-hand corner should be pointing at you. Hold the board down with your left hand, as you would hold a piece of paper while writing. Here you are implanting an idea of correct writing posture.

Now slowly and attentively trace the letter with your index and middle fingers held together, as though you were writing the letter—with the proper form. Watch your own fingers. Your child will too. As you come to the end of the letter, say its sound: *m*. (Notice the interplay of the senses: visual, audio, and tactile.)

Repeat until you think your child can do it himself, then invite him to trace, holding the letter at a slant with his left hand as though he were writing on paper and tracing with right index and middle fingers. If your child is very young or his hand unsure, you may guide his hand smoothly over the letter. Say the sound with him at the end.

Convey a feeling of immense satisfaction: "Wow, here is what it looks like!" This may be old hat to us, but what a revelation to the mind of a child!

Invite your child to repeat the tracing and sound as many times as he likes. Do not hurry him.

When you feel a connection has been firmly established, put the first letter aside and start with the next letter: "Let's think of some words with *a* in them . . . *a*pple . . . *a*stronaut . . . *a*ctor.

Repeat this process until all three letters have been thoroughly introduced.

SECOND PERIOD: *Practicing*

Once you have introduced each of the three letters, review them quickly, still using only the phonetic sound.

"Here is *m*." (Put it down on the table face up.)
"Here is *a*." (Put it down on the table face up.)
"Here is *t*." (Put it down on the table face up.)
"Now I'm going to mix them all up."
    (Make a big show of shuffling.)

Then ask,

"Can you find *t* and trace it?"
"Please put *a* on the shelf."
"I'll close my eyes and you can put *m* in my hands."

If you have more than one child, this part can be very lively. Here your child will get a lot of practice matching the sound and the symbol.

The secret here is that you are not asking your child to tell you the sound, but are providing the new information and asking him to match it with what he knew to begin with. This makes it an easier task—like the difference between a matching quiz and an open-ended question test. In the second period, because you are supplying the sound, it is easier for your child to succeed. Keep on practicing until you are sure he knows which letter belongs to which sound. Only when you are sure he's sure should you go on to the third period.

THIRD PERIOD: *Testing*

Once you are sure your child knows the letter symbol for each sound, make a show of mixing them up again, then place one in front of him and say:

"Trace this and tell me what it says."

Notice tracing is involved in all three periods. The idea of tracing as much as possible is important for the reasons shared before:

- to help the child retain the symbol
- to prepare the hand for writing letters later on

If your child does make a mistake, simply remind him of the correct sound and go on. If, despite a long second period, he seems not to remember the sounds well at all, don't scold. Remember, he's got a long time to learn to read. Simply put the letters away together and repeat the lesson the next day.

Once your child has learned the first three letters, you can put them away until the next lesson—hopefully (though not always possible) the next day. At your second lesson, review the first three letters before introducing the next three. If your child remembers only two, you may substitute the one he has forgotten for one of the new ones, keeping in mind the guidelines for contrast in appearance and sound. Or you may pick it up again later.

If you have a lot on your mind, you may want to keep a list of which letters you've introduced and which ones your child has made his own through memory.

The Word Game

Once he knows eight to ten letters, your child is ready to start forming words. Teaching the entire alphabet of sounds and letters—that is, completing the Sound Game before starting the Word Game—is not only unnecessary but would probably be counterproductive.

So don't wait. Keep the momentum going by introducing the Word Game as soon as your child knows two vowels and six consonants. This new extension of his knowledge will become a powerful incentive in itself. Your child will pick up letters easily as you continue making words together.

With the Word Game, you will be helping your child spell words through breaking them down into component sounds. This is not yet reading, but the most accessible path into reading for the young child. This approach makes the way smooth for reading because it is built on the child's need to start with the concrete, adding the abstract afterwards.

As you help your child form words, he will be hearing and saying the concrete sounds, then finding the abstract symbol. This is much easier for him than looking at letters put together by someone else and trying to abstract the word from them.

You will notice with the Word Game that the child actually "writes" before reading. But since his own motor skills are probably not ready, instead of using a pencil, he will be manipulating a set of letters to put together three-letter phonetic words. (In the meantime, you can help your child perfect his fine motor skills through the activities described in the following box or through exercises I describe in detail in *Small Beginnings*.)

Montessori schools use what is known as a moveable alphabet—a wooden box divided into 26 compartments, one for each letter of the alphabet. As a teacher, once a child was ready to start forming words, I used the box with only the letters the child knew—the other compartments were left empty to avoid confusing the child.

Finger Fitness—Getting Ready to Write

Your child has been getting ready to write since the first Cheerio he picked up between his finger and thumb. Pincer grasp is the key, so anything you give him to help develop that skill will help.

- Puzzles with knobs
- Tweezers
- Sorting small objects
- Coloring books (staying within the lines is a great exercise in control)

More Fun with Letters: Extension Exercises

- Trace letters in a box of damp sand or in Cool Whip, pudding, peanut butter, etc.
- Trace letters in the air with big movements.

It's better to wait until your child has developed some control before giving him paper and pencil to write his own letters. That way he will have a greater chance of success. And you know how much more motivated we are when we see a little success!

At home, there's an even better alternative—magnetic letters. Search for a set with only lowercase letters (of course!) and stick several that your child knows on the refrigerator door. There is no need to have a formal setup for the Word Game, unless you want to. And there's a distinct advantage to having them on the refrigerator door. Although at first you will need to stick close to the letters yourself as you guide your child through the Word Game, later, as your child becomes more independent in forming words himself, you will be able to suggest words to him as you stir the spaghetti or empty the dishwasher.

First Lesson

Gather the letters your child knows, plus one or two new ones. You should be able to make many three-letter phonetic words from them. (The words must be truly phonetic—that is, the letters must stand only for the sounds you have taught.)

Show your child the letters one by one, reviewing the sounds, then placing them on the left side of the refrigerator door (or whatever surface you are working on). Sit on the left side of your child. Now say:

"Let's make some words. How about *'cat'? c . . . a . . . t.*"

Break the word into component sounds. (Remember: say the sound, not the name of the letter.)

"Where is *c*?"

Make a show of looking for the right letter and offering it for his agreement. Then place the letter to the right of the scattered letters at the top left of what will become a column of words.

"*c . . . a . . .*"

As you say *c*, point to it; as you say *a*, point to the space to the right of it. Find the *a* and place it.

"*c . . . a . . . t.*"

Again, point to the sounds as you say them, then the empty space. Find the *t* and place it. Now point to the letters as you say the sounds, several times, each time bringing the sounds closer together. If you have been conscientious about clipping the consonants (saying *c* crisply rather than "cuh"), they will glide together.

"C . . . a . . . t . . . c . . . a . . . t . . . cat."

---

75 Three-Letter Phonetic Words

(There are many more!)

cat	mop	jam	sit	wet
mom	dad	map	can	sip
fat	run	jog	zip	jet
ram	dog	cob	web	pop
cap	rat	bug	hat	lip
rip	jet	gun	hop	hen
pet	bag	yes	hug	hot
rug	let	tub	bag	rub
log	fit	sis	ask	yes
bib	mix	lot	win	jug
men	bit	mob	cab	peg
pig	tax	fun	nod	hum
wag	fix	can	wed	got
lag	did	gum	red	tip
vet	wig	peg	tan	lab

"Now let's make *jam*...*j*...*a*...*m*...*j*...*j*...."

If j is one of the letters your child hasn't learned yet, introduce it:

"This is *j*."

Place it under the *c* as the beginning of the next word on the list you will be making. Go on to finish the word in the same manner as before, reviewing and blending the sounds when complete.

When you feel he is ready, let your child take over finding and placing the letters. Make a list of as many words as you have time for. When you are finished, say something like this:

"Are we finished? Okay, let's go back over the words together."

Now, starting at the top of the list, go back over the words, pointing to the letters and sounding each of them, then blending them together.

Do not ask your child to read the words himself. An important Montessori principle is to make sure a child can succeed before asking him to do something. At this point, a child cannot read.

Keep Practicing

Over the days and weeks to come, as you play the Word Game, you will see your child becoming more independent. You will be able to tell him a word and he will sound it out with less and less help from you. Then it's easy to get a lot of practice because you can give him words no matter how busy you are. Do try to go over his list with him at the end though.

Keep introducing new letters. As your child begins to work more independently, you may slip in a new letter or two and ask him next time to find the ones he doesn't know yet, then give him the sounds. Remember to keep the words phonetic.

Two-Syllable Words Made of Three-Letter Phonetic Parts

magnet	picnic	cobweb	zigzag
basket	pigpen	napkin	sunset

When your child is ready, you can progress (in increasing level of difficulty) to two-syllable words made of three-letter phonetic parts, then four-letter words.

---

50 Four-Letter Phonetic Words

milk	jump	skip	camp	glad
lamp	went	last	wind	club
mend	bent	grab	list	flag
dent	sand	past	brim	clip
damp	lost	spot	tent	plug
rent	flap	west	stop	rust
plan	crop	stem	trip	just
snap	tank	drum	frog	plum
trim	snug	crib	slam	scat
swim	twig	grin	drop	flap

At some point, possibly even while your child is still working on three-letter words, you will notice that he is starting to sound out the words completely on his own. You might say, *"man"* and with little hesitation he will say, *"m . . . a . . . n."*

---

25 Five-Letter Phonetic Words

plant	stamp	split	blast	stand
frost	clamp	brisk	scant	twist
grasp	spilt	scrap	scrub	drift
scram	strip	stung	blend	strum
trust	strap	swung	draft	prong

In this case, don't wait for him to go to four letters or five letters. As soon as you hear this, you know your child is ready to read.

READY TO READ

The Object Game

For your child's first adventure in reading, you will need a basket with five or six small phonetic items you've collected—for instance, a nut, a jet, a pig, a dog, a cat. You will also need slips of paper and a pencil.

For his first introduction to the Object Game, sitting on your child's left, remove all the objects from the basket, naming each as you place it on the table. Now, as your child watches, print the name of one object slowly and carefully on a slip of paper.

Hand the paper to your child and ask, "Can you find this for me?"

Give your child a chance to sound out the word for himself, but if he needs prompting, get him started with the sounds. He should find the object and place the label next to it.

Collectibles for Early Reading

Start a collection of *phonetic* objects—small charms or models that can be used for labeling.

pig	jet	nut	dog	cat
frog	can	pin	peg	bell
bug	lid	top	lock	gum
doll	plug	cap	tack	cup

Collect nonphonetic objects for the next stage. Once your child is comfortable, start introducing these, one at a time, each time he does the Object Game.

fish	spool	penny	dime	jeep
nail	football	boat	shell	lace
soap	chick	fly	spoon	cube
knot	key	flower	bird	bowl

These are just examples, of course. Once you start, you will find yourself building quite a collection. Your children will love labeling these objects.

The key to your child's success here is all the preparation that has come before, plus the limited field of objects from which to choose. He may or may not need a little help, but he should be able to label the objects. Keep the labels in the basket for him to practice with, and as days go by, slip in more objects with corresponding labels.

The Phonetic Object Game works as a transition because it is based on attaching the name to something concrete. But it is just a bridge. As your child gains confidence—"Hey, I can read this one, Mommy!"—he will be able to move easily into the abstract, reading flash cards you make or buy. Use the same sequence with the Object Game as you did with the Word Game:

- three-letter phonetic words
- two-syllable words made of two three-letter phonetic syllables
- four-letter phonetic words
- five-letter phonetic words

NONPHONETIC COMBINATIONS

Now start introducing nonphonetic combinations, for instance, a fish. Help him sound out the word by saying,

"Oh, this is something you need to remember: when *s* and *h* are together, they always say *sh*."

Or in other combinations:

"When you see *ck* together, they just say *c*."

"When two *e*'s are together, they say *ee*."

You may reinforce these common nonphonetic combinations (though with many children you will never need to) with five-by-seven-inch index cards containing lists of printed words with particular combinations.

One combination per card. Use red markers to write the combinations, black for the other letters. Other nonphonetic combinations include *th* (two sounds, as in *th*is and brea*th*), *ow* (two sounds, as in b*ow*l and *ow*l), *qu, ou, oi, oy, kn, gn.* Keep in mind that for most readers you will not need to make a card for every sound. For the best readers you will not need cards at all; they will learn the exceptions as they read.

Sample Nonphonetic Combination Cards

ee	oo	i_e	a_e	ai
feet	moon	mine	late	pail
see	soon	tire	same	rain
week	tool	hide	tale	maid
teen	scoot	file	wade	fair
keep	balloon	bite	fake	nail
reed	raccoon	hive	pane	wait
peel	boot	wife	maze	waist
ay	ch	y	y	o_e
say	chip	baby	cry	hole
day	chest	penny	sky	poke
may	chop	bunny	try	rope
play	chug	skinny	fry	home
stay	inch	funny	my	dome
way	chick	silly	fly	note
ray	bench	holy	empty	voter

When you introduce a card to your child, explain, for example:

"When you see two *o*'s together, they say *oo*."

Then go over the words one by one, helping him read *oo* instead of *o . . . o*.

Puzzle Words

Create a set of "puzzle words" for your child. Old business cards are the perfect size (and price), plus it's easy to wrap a rubber band around them. On the back of each, print a word that has no logical reason to be spelled the way it is, but that is essential to our vocabulary.

Puzzle Words		
you	I	are
our	the	why
eye	oh	sew
have	some	busy
what	one	two
once	come	done
both	they	were
was	four	put

These are just some examples. There are plenty more!

Puzzle words must be taught by sight. You might explain:

"There are some words we just can't sound out. We just have to know them when we see them."

Teach puzzle words in groups of three, using the Three Period Lesson format. Pop them in your purse or coat jacket on your way to the pediatrician's office or any place you'll have a couple of minutes to sit. Then you can use them like flash cards with your child to make your waiting time worthwhile.

LET IT FLOW

Hold on to your hat! The powerful spark ignited when your child makes his first reading breakthrough (as with the phonetic object game, the first time he "gets" it) will amaze and humble you as your child "explodes" into reading.

Think of how your child learned to speak. Starting with only a few words, somewhere between two and three he exploded into full language. You didn't have to teach him every word or proper sentence structure. God built that capacity for speech development into him.

God also built the capacity to communicate through the written word into him. Once a child succeeds at reading phonetically, with very little help he will explode into reading, picking up books, and enjoying the challenge of figuring out new words himself. Just as much as your child wanted to communicate through his own spoken words, he will want to read the words in all those wonderful books you have provided and read to him.

Because of your child's motivation, you will not need to teach him every rule and every exception to perfect his reading skills. Just as he learned to speak through exposure to spoken language, he will learn to read through exposure to books.

Now the greatest part of your work is over—and it really didn't seem that much like work after all, did it?

You have prepared your child well. The rest of the work will be his. In the next chapter I will share more ways to exercise his reading skills. But believe me, your child will be having so much fun, it will never seem like work at all.

Remember, a well-prepared child has confidence, and the thrill of being able to read is a powerful motivator. At this stage, you will have to do little coaxing. Once you initiate a young child into reading, he will usually take over the controls himself.

READING TIPS

If you've read board books to your baby, then left them in easy reach, you've already discovered books have great drawing power, even for little ones. My little guys, Daniel and Jesse, can often be found poring over the pages of a board book they've enjoyed with Mom or Dad—or big brother or sister!

By the time he is two or three, you should be able to trust your child with other books—the kind with paper pages—as well. The key is to prepare him carefully, by instilling a high regard for reading and a reverence for books.

I mentioned before the importance of your child seeing you read. In addition to reading to him, find times to read side-by-side—you engrossed in your book while he "reads" his. Make it a habit to take children's books with you everywhere—to the doctor's office, the beach, or Grandma's; on the bus, short trips, or vacation. Read in the morning, before naps, after dinner, and before bed. Be careful never to make it seem like a chore, but like a refreshing break, something you look forward to wholeheartedly.

Take trips to the library and the bookstore. When you've watched a movie that originated as a book, check the book out of the library. Your child will be impressed to know a video he loves began as a book.

Make sure your child sees the practical applications of reading. Point out highway signs, labels on cereal boxes, maps, newspapers, telephone directories, and cookbooks. When the mail comes, read the names and addresses on the envelope to show him who it's for and who it's from. Read the mail to him. Emphasize that reading is an important way we have to *communicate.*

Have lots of books in the house, as well as snuggly places to read. Make your child's solo reading extra special by creating a reading nook. It doesn't require much area (after all, a child isn't very big!)—a cozy chair or maybe just a large comfy pillow on the floor next to a sunny window. Decorate the area with some small pictures hung at her level. Place an inexpensive bookcase (or make your own by covering sturdy boxes with contact paper) to hold her own books.

Begin early to teach your child how to handle books with respect. (If you grew up in a home where books were used for coasters, you might want to rethink this now that you're paying for them yourself!) When you read with your child, exaggerate the care with which you turn the pages. Teach your child when he is finished reading a book to place it upright on the shelf with the binding facing out.

Start a book by reading the title and the author with your child. This lets her know that a book is someone's creation. You might want to talk about the cover art, and mention the name of the artist. This lets her know that a book is a collaborative effort.

Start early to help your child make the distinction between reality and fantasy. There are three kinds of books:

- stories that really happened (the Bible, historical accounts)
- stories that could happen (as in *Ira Sleeps Over,* a dilemma any child could face)

- stories that could never happen at all (*Where the Wild Things Are*)

Some people question using fantasy at all with children. Montessori did; she felt that toddlers—because they could not think abstractly—could not distinguish between fantasy and reality. Besides, she reasoned, reality is so full of marvelous things, that we can easily fill the early years just teaching children all the wonders of the world, saving fantasy for later.

Likewise, some parents, for religious reasons, wish to avoid fantasy, or even stories that have animals as talking characters.

I see value in fantasy, although it requires an extra amount of discernment on the part of parents to make sure that the author's message—because every author has one—is compatible with what they want their children to learn. Books with animal characters (I especially think of Russell Hoban's *Frances* books) can teach important lessons in charming and nonthreatening ways. Through projecting the child's conflicts and fears—for instance the birth of a sibling—onto something safe (like a whimsical raccoon) the author helps children cope. Books like *Where the Wild Things Are*, which some Christian parents might reject, deal with very real and inexpressible childhood feelings, showing them resolved, with security restored at the end.

Remember, at this age a child cannot think abstractly. Therefore, the only way you can teach him about courage, loyalty, faith, and love is through stories.

Christian parents can get more out of books that are not specifically Christian through discussion in which they apply

Christian themes. That way they are also teaching their children that their spirituality does not exist in a vacuum. It's not tied to specific times and books. It is a filter through which they can view any information that comes their way.

But back to reading the story itself. You can read three ways:

1. Comprehensively: spending time on each page to discuss and ask questions
2. Technically: noting sentences, words, letters ("Do you see an *s* on this page?")
3. Dramatically: presenting material uninterruptedly, with focus only on the story, holding any questions or comments until the end

It's a good idea to do some reading each way, though the first and third are how you'll spend most of your reading time.

Above all, have a good time! Reading with your child can be tremendously freeing, especially if you've always wanted to be a little less reserved! Now's the time to be dramatic. Any parent can be Oscar-worthy in the eyes of an admiring child. Make stories come alive through variations in tempo, pitch, or inflection. Create character voices, make background noises, and use hands and arms to illustrate emotions.

Since you will be reading stories more than once (I figured out I've read *Go, Dog, Go* at least six hundred times), you might as well make them as enjoyable as you can for yourself!

BOOK RECOMMENDATIONS
Two To Five Years

Bedtime for Frances (also *A Baby Sister for Frances, A Birthday for Frances*, etc.), Russell Hoban, HarperCollins, 1976

You will surely fall in love with Frances, the raccoon who brings the problems of childhood to life in such a warm and whimsical way. Frances' mother and father are always there to help her through her latest crisis, with serenity and a sense of humor.

The Bible Illustrated for Little Children, Ella K. Lindvall, Moody Press, 1985

Walk through the Bible with your child—from creation to Paul's imprisonment—with these gorgeously illustrated, captivatingly told one-page stories. Each story is followed by conversational questions. A beautiful way to begin building a foundation.

The Carrot Seed, Ruth Krauss, Trophy Press, 1945

A little boy plants a seed, and though he receives a lot of discouragement, he does all he can to help it grow. His efforts are rewarded.

Cat in the Hat (also *Fox in Socks* and *Green Eggs and Ham*), Dr. Seuss, Random House, 1957

One of the best parts of being a parent is getting to revisit old favorites like these. These funny, fantastic books beg to be read over and over. Later, because they are as close as best friends, they will become confidence builders as your child begins to read.

Corduroy, Don Freeman, Viking, 1968

A stuffed bear wants a home, but waiting in the department store has taken its toll. Still, a little girl falls in love with him. A tale about security and unconditional love.

Giant Steps for Little People, Kenneth N. Taylor, Tyndale, 1985

The Sermon on the Mount and the Ten Commandments, broken into "bite-sized morsels a very young child can grasp and grow on." Each page offers a spiritual truth, a practical application (with lots of opportunities for parent-child conversation), a prayer, and a memory verse. A treasure.

Go, Dog, Go, Philip D. Eastman, Random House, 1961

One of the silliest teaching books around, this book is jam-packed with adjectives and prepositions—important for later skills—but is still guaranteed to give your child a fun time. Another book that will eventually double as an early reader.

Ira Sleeps Over, Bernard Waber, Houghton Mifflin Co., 1973

How exciting to be invited to spend the night at a friend's house—but how scary to face the prospect of sleeping without your teddy bear! A childhood dilemma depicted with empathy and humor.

Just in Case You Ever Wonder, Max Lucado, Word, 1992

A sort of a "have I told you lately that I love you statement" from parent to child, this tender book will build your child's sense of peace and protection. A tender reminder that you are always there for him—and so is God.

A Light on the Path: Proverbs for Growing Wise, L. J. Sattgast, Multnomah Press, 1996

Proverbs set to rhyme. Charmingly illustrated for children.

The Little Engine that Could, Watty Piper, Platt & Munck, 1930

A wonderful message for children: With a humble heart and a little determination, even the smallest can save the day. A classic for generations.

The Little Red Hen, various authors and publishers since 1942

Hooray for a good work ethic! The little red hen asks but receives no help in her efforts to put bread on the table. Yet all who wouldn't help would like to eat. In a refreshingly old-fashioned triumph of moral consequences, they don't get to.

Madeline, Ludwig Bemelmans, Viking, 1958.

A classic told in charming rhyme, this book opens the window to a different world, where little French girls go to boarding school and one has her appendix removed.

Make Way for Ducklings, Robert McCloskey, Viking, 1941

Such a family-values story! Mr. and Mrs. Mallard search for the perfect spot to raise their family, with some assistance from a friendly police officer. Told and illustrated with humor and warmth.

Millions of Cats, Wanda Gag, various publishers since 1928

An enchanting tale of a man who comes home with "hundreds of cats, thousands of cats, millions and billions and trillions of cats." Lots of rhythm, rhyme, and repetition make a strong point: Humility can keep you from harm and love can bring out beauty.

My Very First Book of Bible Words, Mary Hollingsworth, Thomas Nelson, 1993

A child's faith vocabulary: Words like *worship, obey, family,* and *church,* are illustrated and made real through brief definitions, Bible quotes, and activities.

Noah's Ark, Peter Spier, Doubleday, 1977

This award-winning version of the Bible story is accompanied by sparkling, intricate, and highly satisfying illustrations. Your child will love the details.

Peter's Chair, Ezra Jack Keats, Trophy Press, 1967

Peter faces life with a new sister—including all his furniture being painted pink. How will he learn to accept his new place in the family?

Play with Me, Marie Hall Ets, Viking, 1955

On my first read of this book, I found it a little too quiet—but that's the point. Children must get it, because they seem fascinated by this tale of a lonely girl who finds friends in the forest through cultivating patience and stillness. After reading, challenge your child to be still and quiet. A great lesson in self-control.

The Puppy Who Wanted a Boy, Jane Thayer, Scholastic, 1968

Petey the puppy wants a boy for Christmas, but his mother tells him he'll have to find one on his own. Of course there's a happy ending!

The Rainbow Fish, Marcus Pfister, Scholastic, 1992

A new tale destined to become a classic. The story of a beautiful, proud, and selfish little fish who discovers life isn't much fun without sharing. A finely drawn message just right for children. The editions that have real glittery scales shimmer too!

Stone Soup, Ann McGovern, Scholastic, 1968

The hilarious tale of an old woman and the clever vagabond who convinces her that she can make soup from a stone, while persuading her to add a little of this and a little of that. Children love this story—and then making soup afterward.

When I'm a Mommy, Ginger Adair Fulton, Moody Press, 1984

A sweet addition to the spiritual life of any little girl, this retelling of Proverbs 31 will give her much to look forward to!

Where the Wild Things Are, Maurice Sendak, Harper and
   Row, 1963

   The wildly imaginative tale of a boy, sent to his room
with no supper, who finds his way through an emotional
jungle filled with funny looking monsters—then back to
his own room. Reaffirms the old notion that there's just
no place like home!

Chapter Three
READ!
Five to Seven Years

*A*llison *could hardly believe it! Her little girl was really read-*
ing! Once Tina began reading phonetic words and match-
ing them to the objects, in just a week or so she was able to read
the words all by themselves. Then, before Allison could even
think about what to do next, Tina was picking up Go, Dog,
Go, *and reading it by herself.*

It seemed like only yesterday when they had first started
doing the Sound Game together. The magnetic letters were still
on the refrigerator door; Tina still enjoyed sounding out words.
Allison had also started her on writing the letters, something for
which Tina was now well prepared because of all her practice
with the Letter Game.

Allison wasn't worried anymore about whether Tina would
be ready for school. "I worry more about how ready school will
be for her," she laughed with her mother-in-law. Allison and
Steve were still praying, trying to make the right decision about
where to send Tina to school.

Steve, surprisingly, had become pretty enthusiastic about the
idea of home school. He was so impressed that Allison had been

able to teach Tina to read—and that Tina could not only read beautifully, but loved to read as well.

Steve said it meant a lot to him to know that the mother of his children had so much to give. Allison had to admit that she hadn't been too sure in the beginning, but now, well—a lot of things seemed doable that she had never thought of before. She was even starting to teach Tina a little math. Plus they were learning the names of trees and the instruments in the orchestra.

Now when they went shopping together, Allison would offer Tina a book as a treat, rather than a toy or candy. The huge discount stores carried early reader books for just a few dollars. They were building up a nice little library of their own. Even though Tina would be graduating quickly to more advanced books, Allison knew there would be other readers in the house someday.

In fact, she and Steve were currently working on that.

◆　◆　◆　◆

This will be the shortest chapter, for in getting your child off to a lifelong love of reading, there's not much left for you to do.

Once your child begins to read, especially when he's learned in a natural manner appropriate to his age level, his reading will continue to improve with little effort on your part—as long as he continues to read.

And you should experience few problems with a young child who finds himself able to read, choosing to read.

As he reads, your child will encounter all the exceptions and strangely constructed words that we have postponed while taking the phonetic approach. However, because of his success with phonetic reading, your child will tackle these words with confidence. He will develop word-attack skills through

- the systematic or casual introduction of nonphonetic combinations
- a growing sight vocabulary (words not decipherable any other way)
- figuring out words in context

Given plenty of reading material, a child can actually develop an impressive vocabulary, perfect grammar, and excellent spelling—all on his own.

But just to make sure, and to keep a hand in the development of her reading skills, here are some ideas to keep her moving along.

DEVELOPING READING SKILLS

Recognizing Words

Your child enjoyed the Phonetic Object Game, labeling a basketful of objects. As his word-attack skills increase, you can give him labels for everything in sight—window, door, chair, couch, sink.

If you want to invest a little more time and effort, check the hardware department for organizers with little plastic drawers. Then label a drawer for every room in your house and fill each drawer with labels for the contents of that particular room.

Write action words on slips of paper and have your child read and perform the action—hop, skip, walk, run, twirl, dance, glide, slide, spin, shuffle, bounce, dart, zoom, march, roll, strut, plod, trudge, flit, race. This can be a vocabulary builder too!

If you are reading a magazine or book that is too advanced for her reading level, challenge her to find words on the page that she knows. Look for words she knows on labels, on the highway, and in the mail.

Understanding What Words Do

At the same time, keep increasing his awareness of how words are used in our language. From the labeling, he knows that some words name things. He also has a sense, through using his whole body, that some words involve action.

Now you can begin to draw her attention to words that describe things:

"How many words can we think of to tell us more about this bunny?" (gray, little, soft, quiet, fluffy, squirmy, etc.)

Adjectives: Words That Describe

<u>size</u>	<u>color</u>	<u>shape</u>	<u>properties</u>	<u>texture</u>	<u>feelings</u>	<u>characteristics</u>
big	red	round	heavy	smooth	sad	quiet
small	blue	square	light	rough	happy	wiggly
huge	green	triangular	solid	bumpy	mad	fast
teeny	yellow	rectangular	bouncy	slippery	worried	slow
gigantic	pink	pointed	cold	prickly	excited	noisy

By now you get the picture. Our language is loaded with adjectives. Use them with your sweet, excited, wiggly, teachable, loveable, indispensable little ones!

Show him how some words show relationship:

"Here is a little black pebble. Can you put it *on* the table? *under* the table? *beside* the table?

Prepositions: Words that Show Relationship

above	before	between	inside	over
against	behind	by	near	under
around	below	from	off	with
at	beside	in	on	without

This is a partial list, appropriate for five- to seven-year-olds.

Here you will be laying the groundwork for future language studies, giving your child experience with how words work in our language. He will benefit from this later when he learns the parts of speech; nouns, verbs, adjectives, and prepositions.

Make sure your child understands the way we use comparatives and superlatives:

"Which shirt is larger—this one or that one?"

"Which of these three balls is the biggest? the smallest?"

Now's also the time to start asking him about:

- rhyming words
- synonyms (words that mean the same)
- antonyms (words that mean the opposite)
- homonyms (words that sound the same but have different spellings and meanings)

However, at this point you don't use those terms. Just ask:

"Can you think of a word that rhymes with tell?"
"What is the opposite of hot?"
"Is there a word that means the same thing as big?"
"The wind *blew* a *blue* kite. Are there two words that sound the same?"

Working with Letters

Continue to work on writing skills. Begin by teaching your child proper writing posture. Make sure he has a child-friendly place to write, something that takes his smaller size into consideration. He needs a stable, smooth writing surface and to have his feet resting firmly on something solid. Show him how to tilt the paper so that the bottom left corner is pointing at his belly button. Show him how to use his left hand to hold the paper in position (see appendix I for instructions for lefties). Show him how to lean forward slightly and how to move his writing arm across the paper.

Begin with the letters that are easiest to form (*l, o, i, c*). Write one per line on lined paper (preferably the elementary-ruled wide sheets). Let your child trace around the letter you have written, then continue making them on his own. Encourage him to keep trying by saying something like, "Let's try to make each one a little more beautiful than the last." To help a child with weaker motor skills, fill the line yourself with letters of dotted lines. Then he can trace around the dots.

Once your child has practiced a number of letters, he can begin to write phonetic words instead of using the magnetic letters. Show him how to leave a space between words on a line.

Since your child will not need uppercase letters until he is writing sentences, you can wait until that time to have him practice writing them. By then he will have come across them one at a time in his own reading, so they will be familiar.

Your child may have already picked up from *Sesame Street* or elsewhere that besides sounds, letters also have names. Some children have no difficulty with memorizing both simultaneously; but for others it's a stretch. For the latter it's especially important not to burden them with memorizing names until after reading is established. Then you can teach the names of letters, explaining, "You know this letter makes the sound *rrr*. The name of the letter is *R*."

Now's the time to teach the alphabet in sequence. If it seems late, because every three-year-old on your street knows the alphabet song, think about it; the only reason we need to know the alphabet in sequence is to look things up in the dictionary—a skill the child isn't introduced to until at least second grade.

Expanding Vocabulary

Through reading and conversation, try to give your child the richest vocabulary you can. At this point you should be talking to your child—at least in terms of the words you choose—the same way you would talk to an adult.

A broad vocabulary not only expands the child's mastery of his environment, it also expands his ability to perceive. When we go by a construction site and comment on the commotion, the powerful equipment, the workers' skill, and the effect on the surrounding buildings, we stir our children's imagination and attention to detail. It's like opening windows in their minds.

Try to reach beyond words like *nice, good, bad, okay,* for ones that more accurately describe how things are. Offer verbal fill-in-the-blanks:

"Red is a color that looks so _____."
"When my dog sees me, he acts _____."

When your child is caught up in an emotion, give him the name for it:

"Are you feeling jealous?"

Now it's time to start attaching those abstract words like *courage, faith,* and *loyalty* to the stories you're reading. Just remember, they will only have meaning if they are linked to something specific in the child's mind.

Stimulating Creativity

If we want our children to have a healthy curiosity about life and living—which is what will make them better readers and better learners—we need to encourage this in the early years.

Talk with your child about everything. Look at him while he talks. Through your questions, encourage him to make the most of his observation, thinking, and reasoning skills. Ask open-ended questions:

Not: "Did you have a good time at the park?"
But: "What did you enjoy about the park today?"

When your child draws a picture, ask him to tell you about it and let him watch you as you write his words on the picture. Show him that this is like making a book. In fact, he can draw many pictures and you can staple them together to make his own book. You can write the story on the pages as he tells it to you.

Another fun project you can do with your child is to start a diary with him—before he can write it himself. Explain to him what a diary is all about, how it helps us to remember important things we've done or people we've met or feelings we've had. Then open the diary with him each day and ask him what he would like you to write down for him.

Providing Enrichment

Provide your child with as much exposure as possible to art and music—not just his own hands-on efforts, but encounters with the classics.

Small art reproductions (easy to find in greeting card form) hung at his eye level offer opportunities for many open-ended questions, encouraging your child to think and use his imagination. Boys especially love Winslow Homer's work; the boys playing crack-the-whip and the fishermen racing home before the storm are rich in conversation possibilities.

I didn't grow up with much exposure to classical music myself, but I have enjoyed learning a little as an adult. Playing some Mozart or Haydn can have an incomparable calming effect on a day that's gotten a little too rowdy. And did you know that studies show that just listening to classical music boosts IQ levels?

My children and I get up half an hour earlier than we have to just to sing some hymns together before we start our day. The poetry is so beautiful; I often draw inspiration from a line of a hymn and make an on-the-spot devotional. As I once heard Florence Littauer say, "Where two or more children are gathered, Mom will teach a lesson."

Read poetry and memorize it with your children. Sing lots of songs—all types of songs—with them. Don't worry about your voice. They are sure to think it's the most beautiful voice in the world. (Where else will you find such an appreciative audience?) Try to sing every day.

Don't do it because you should; do it because it's fun!

Developing Humor

Since your baby's first laugh, hasn't his sense of humor been special to you? Don't his giggles and guffaws still make your heart merry? Keep them coming and motivate your early reader to read a little extra by using joke and riddle books from the library. Each of my children in their earliest reading days enjoyed reading riddles to me.

"Why did the chicken cross the road?
"To get to the other side." (Hey, this is easy.)
"Why did the gumball cross the road?"
"Why?" (Obviously someone's been doing some thinking to keep us parents on our toes!)
"Because it was stuck to the chicken's foot!"

Humorous poetry and tongue twisters are sure to grab his attention as well.

As your child matures, he will begin to appreciate more subtle humor, especially with you beside him to smile at the appropriate moments. For instance, I've always found the description of the little duck's family in *The Story about Ping* to be hilarious—maybe because of our big family. Simply through your voice inflection, you can highlight the humor in the books you read with your child.

Ordering Reality

It is largely through language that we are able to perceive the order in the universe. A child of four or five is beginning to understand that life is not random. This is the appropriate time to give him all the language he needs to understand weather, seasons, days of the weeks, months of the year, and times of the day.

Give him a beginning sense of classification skills with the following fun game. Sort toys into various groups:

- stuffed toys
- building toys
- toys made of wood/plastic/metal
- toys with wheels/immovable toys
- toys you play with indoors/outdoors
- toys you play with by yourself/with friends
- large toys/small toys
- toys that need batteries/toys that don't
- toys with one part/toys with many

Stretch your child in his ability to think sequentially.

Begin with one or two directions, either fun or useful:

"Skip to the end of our sidewalk and twirl three times."
"Please take this bowl to the kitchen and bring me a dish
    towel."

Then, as your child shows he can successfully carry out
the directions, begin adding more at a time.

"Shut your eyes, then wiggle your nose, then turn around,
    and sit down."
"Please get out your lunchbox, put in a container of
    yogurt from the fridge, a banana, a spoon, and a nap-
    kin."

Building your child's skills in classification and following
directions gives him a feeling of security—through understanding and participating in the order around him.

Perfecting Grammar

By the time a child is four or five, he has mastered the
basic structure of his language. The grammar mistakes your
child might be making at this point are more subtle than the
obvious ones he made as a toddler, often errors a significant
number of adults make as well. You will want your child to
be conscious of the correction, but you can do it in a positive
way by a technique called mirroring:

"Her and I want to go to the store."
"Her and I?"
"She and I."

"Our team didn't do so good today."
"Didn't do so good or didn't do so well?"
"Didn't do so well."

If your own grammar could use a brush-up, all you need is a good, traditional fifth-grade language workbook, such as the one published by A Beka Books, a book source in appendix E.

Reinforcing Basics

"What do you think about workbooks?" is one of the questions I hear frequently. My answer? I love workbooks.

I think workbooks have gotten a bad rap in recent years because of the de-emphasis on structure in public schools. I have met a lot of teachers who have few kind words for workbooks, yet the truth is, I have never met a child who didn't like them.

I said earlier that a child will pick up all the rules, exceptions, and outrageous things about our language just through reading. Still, it never hurts to make sure he's seen it all. And for a slower learner, a phonics workbook will break reading components into bite-sized pieces, boosting the child's confidence as he makes a little progress each day.

A good phonics workbook is an invaluable asset in sharpening your child's language skills. I have my own favorites, which I share in appendix J.

Giving Encouragement

The greatest asset your child has in her early reading days is you. Your praise and encouragement will give your child confidence and a sense of security as she tries her wings. She needs to know you have faith in her abilities. As long as she has confidence, she will be eager to keep reading.

Never label a child or make her feel inadequate. An encouraging word goes a long way.

> "I know this might seem hard to you now—it does to a lot of kids who learn to read. Don't worry. In a few days you'll know it so well you'll never remember that you thought it was hard."

Some children do need more time and practice than others. If you have a slower learner, rather than feeling frustrated or self-critical, be grateful that you are teaching her yourself—these are the children who especially need to be taught at home. At school, without the one-on-one attention, they'd just slip through the cracks.

Teaching Tips

What works:	What doesn't work:
Patience	Impatience
Confidence	Expectations
Flexibility	that are too high
Ability to assess child's	Distractions
strengths and	Lack of sensitivity to
weaknesses	child's limits

Remember: *Prayer does wonders for the child you teach and for you as well!*

Getting the Whole Picture

So much of reading is not just deciphering words on the page, but what we bring to the experience ourselves. Part of enabling your child to become the best reader he can be is building up his language skills in every way you can.

The areas I've mentioned so far—recognizing words, building vocabulary, perfecting grammar, and reinforcing basics—are all part of the package your child brings to the experience of reading. The stronger he is in these areas, the more capable a reader he will be; the more capable a reader he is, the more he will enjoy reading; the more he enjoys reading, the stronger he will be in all these areas—grammar, vocabulary and—well, by now you get the picture, I'm sure.

Anything we can do to build our children's language or reading skills will spill over into all the other areas. So even if you only have time to do a little, do a little. In the area of language, as in all of parenting, a little means a lot.

Introducing Readers

Now comes the fun part—introducing readers. When I first started teaching twenty-some years ago, this was the hardest area for us as teachers. We'd get our kids all ready for phonetic reading, and then there just weren't any interesting phonetic readers available.

That's not a problem now. There are shelves of early reader books out there, and some good writers are writing thoroughly enjoyable stories for early readers.

I start out with *Bob Books* (see end of chapter), which are almost completely phonetic and begin with only a few words and a cute drawing on each page. This gets the child used to the idea that sentences

- are composed of words and spaces;
- begin with capital letters;
- end with periods;
- often contain sight words like *a* and *the.*

At the same time, they boost any child's confidence by making it possible for him to read a whole book by himself. What a wonderful job these authors have done!

Now the secret about reading is this: Getting a child ready is where most of the work goes on. And each stage can take different amounts of time for different children. Some children take a long time of playing the Sound Game before they "get it"—that words are made up of individual sounds. Some children take a long time making the connection between the sound and the symbol. But even if a child has spent a lot of time at any particular prereading stage, don't assume that his explosion into reading will be slow.

In the beginning of this book, I shared my experience with my daughter Sophia, whose developmental timetable was over a year behind what I had come to expect through all my work with children. Though she didn't read until she was seven, within six months she was reading at second grade level.

My son Zachary seemed to take forever to pick up ten letters so that we could start phonetic combinations. Yet once he did, at age five and one-half, within a year he was reading at third grade level. By eight he was reading at tenth grade level. Don't limit your child's progress by labeling him as slow just because he took a little longer in one area than you might have expected.

I insert this caveat here because sometimes the shift from reading one word at a time to reading sentences fluently can take a little time. You may have to sit through many readings of *Bob Books* before you see the results you want. If this is the case, be patient. Keep building up your child in all the other areas of language skills discussed previously. Keep reading books to him. And keep encouraging him. At some point—provided your child has not become discouraged and given up—as though you had reached the top of the roller coaster, your child will begin zooming down a track of his own. Reading will become easy and fun.

A world of wonderful early readers is waiting for him (see end of chapter). He will also begin reading some of the books that have become best friends through all the hours you've spent reading aloud. Books like *The Cat in the Hat*, *Green Eggs and Ham*, and *Go, Dog, Go* are perfect confidence builders. Because the child knows them well, he will be able to figure out many sight words and make them his own.

Be careful not to give your child books above his reading level. It's a good idea to keep stretching him vocabulary-wise, but in the early reading days more than a few unfamiliar words per page are too many.

Building Comprehension

Make the most of your child's experience with early readers by building his reading comprehension. Instead of closing the book and putting it away when you're finished, ask questions about:

- the main idea
- the order and sequence of events
- the characters
- the setting
- the important details

Ask him to summarize:

"What happened in the story?"

Encourage him to make judgments:

"Did you think the boy did the right thing?"
"What would you have done?"
"Why did you like the story?"

Reading Aloud

Just because your child is reading solo, don't stop reading aloud. And though you are careful to make sure that the books he reads himself are at his reading level, your own reading to your child can be well above—in fact, the same as yours.

For fourteen years my husband, Tripp, has read nightly to our children, including many classics *(Treasure Island, David Copperfield)* and works as sophisticated as *The Lord of the Rings* trilogy. In listening to stories, your child does not have to understand every word. He will absorb the richness of the language and a lot of meaning simply through context and the drama with which you read.

In addition, this early experience of listening to a grown-up read grown-up literature establishes a pattern of how the child will read when he reads to himself. If he has first heard the classics read with enthusiasm and emotion, he will bring these qualities to his own reading later on.

His comprehension will be better also. A child who has spent a lot of time concentrating and listening will find it easy to read without submitting to distractions from within or without. He'll be able to follow the author's thoughts page after page.

Perhaps most of all, he will bring to his reading experience all the warmth and good feeling that is his through the special moments shared with the people most important to him in all the world—his parents.

Tripp's nightly reading has not only built a special bond between him and the children, but also between our children and good literature. Our family life has been greatly enriched by the cozy hours he has spent.

Think of this: In twenty years no one will remember whether you finished cleaning up before you went to bed each night. Neither will they remember if you solved that programming problem or landed that important customer. But your children will always remember the books you read, the talks you had, and the lessons they learned at your knee.

Both Tripp and I can say with assurance that you will look back on the times you have spent reading to your children as some of the best-spent hours of your life.

READING TIPS

Books for this age are so exciting! What a wonder that simply by turning the pages of a book we can give our children an up close and personal look at life on the other side of the globe, or the other side of the century! Or serve up a tale meant to help him cope with his problems or build his character. Or share with him our history or your faith.

Your five- to seven-year-old is now ready to be introduced to an abundance of life—the broadest spectrum of races, places, cultures, and historical periods. He needs to know that in our own country, even in our own home town, not everyone lives the same way. Especially if your child lives in comfortable circumstances, he needs to know that others live in need.

He also needs to know that material circumstances don't say much at all about the things that truly make life worth living. As in *A Chair for My Mother*, a family can go through many ups and downs and yet find great joy in something small and simple.

Building values start earlier than we might think. At five years old, children are really beginning to size up the world and the adults around them. They have a lot of questions regarding right and wrong. They want answers.

At this age, the most appropriate way to teach values is through stories. In *The Little Red Lighthouse and the Great Gray Bridge*, children see pride projected onto a protagonist that isn't even human. This makes it safe to look at. Remember, Jesus taught grown-ups by parables about real situations, not by abstract talks about virtues. We can do the same with our children.

When possible, preview a book before reading it with your child, so you can make sure you understand the message. Every writer has an agenda. When we read a book to our children, we need to know that the agenda behind it is compatible with our own. Of course, this means that you also need to be very clear about your own agenda.

Whatever you do, don't leave your child empty, to absorb the values of popular culture, television, and movies. Take a proactive approach. Have a plan. Decide what's important to your family and then back it up by making sure that the books you give your child, as well as the shows you let him watch, are compatible with your values.

If in doubt, skip it. There's too much good stuff out there to waste time on books that undermine the values you hold dear. Seek out those books that will stretch you and your child in a positive direction.

BOOK RECOMMENDATIONS
Five to Seven Years

READ-ALOUD STORIES

Alexander and the Terrible, Horrible, No Good, Very Bad Day,
Judith Viorst, Aladdin, 1972

Everyone has a really bad day now and then. Alexander gives us a language for sharing it and accepting it. Contemporary and funny.

Blueberries for Sal, Robert McCloskey, Puffin Books, 1948

What happens when a little girl and a little bear wander away from their blueberry-picking mothers and switch who they follow? A beautifully illustrated story sets a lovely mood, then introduces just enough suspense for children.

A Chair for My Mother, Vera B. Williams, Mulberry, 1982

A remarkably beautiful story told by a young girl whose mother is a waitress. Since they lost all their furniture in a fire, they've been saving Mother's tips in a jar so they can buy a big comfortable chair for their whole family to enjoy—daughter, mother, and grandmother. Life has its ups and downs, but there's always lots of love.

Frog and Toad Are Friends (and other *Frog and Toad* books),
Arnold Lobel, HarperCollins, 1970

A pair of loveable best friends spend the summer watching out for and bringing out the best in each other. Doubles as an early reader.

George Shrinks, William Joyce, Scholastic, 1985

Nothing heavy, just a romp for the imagination when George dreams he is small and wakes up the size of a peanut. Your child will love the pictures in which George flies for the mail in a toy airplane.

Goops and How to Be Them: A Manual of Manners for Polite Infants Inculcating Many Juvenile Virtues Both by Precept and Example, with 90 Drawings (also *More Goops*), Gelett Burgess, Dover Publications, republished 1968

"The Goops they lick their fingers, and the Goops they lick their knives; they spill their broth on tablecloth—Oh, they lead disgusting lives!" This old-fashioned compendium of poems on manners is just plain hilarious—and one of the easiest ways to teach children manners.

Harold and the Purple Crayon, Crockett Johnson, HarperCollins, 1955

An ingenious tale. Harold goes out for a walk with a purple crayon in his hand, and draws himself all kinds of adventures, showing some common sense and good problem-solving skills along the way.

The Hole in the Dike, retold by Norma Green, Scholastic, 1974

As the author states at the end of the book, this tale was spun a hundred years ago by a woman who had never been to Holland. Yet it so symbolized the struggle of the Dutch that they erected a statue to the boy who saved his country from floods. A tale that underscores sacrifice and loyalty to one's country.

Least of All, Carol Purdy, Aladdin, 1987

The youngest of six children—and the only girl—Raven Hannah is not big enough to help with any of the work on her family's farm. But when she teaches herself to read from the Bible, she finds that as the first reader in the family, she has a unique gift to offer.

The Lion and the Mouse, A. J. Wood, illustrated by Ian Andrew, Millbrook Press, 1995

Aesop's classic fable, beloved by readers throughout the ages, of a mighty lion who spares the life of a mouse and is amply repaid for his mercy.

The Little House, Virginia Lee Burton, Scholastic, 1942

"Once upon a time there was a little house way out in the country. She was a pretty Little House and she was strong and well built." The contrast between the Little House's peaceful existence with the beautiful seasons and her life when a big city grows around her makes for a touching tale. The deeper theme: Progress has a price. Children will love the pictures, the happy ending, and the lesson learned by the Little House.

Little People in Tough Spots: Bible Answers for Young Children, V. Gilbert Beers, Thomas Nelson, 1992

This gem of a book shows children in an easy-to-understand way that the answers to life's problems are in the Bible. Pick a problem—"I'm scared," "I have too much to do," "Do I have to share?"—and you will find a vignette of a present-day child who faces the problem, then draws inspiration from a particular person in the Bible.

The Little Red Lighthouse and the Great Gray Bridge,
   Hildegarde H. Swift, Harcourt Brace, 1942
   A little lighthouse on the Hudson River starts out with a little too much pride, suffers great humiliation when the George Washington Bridge is built, and finally gains a properly modest confidence when it finds that it is useful and has an important job to do.

Ox-Cart Man, Donald Hall, Viking Press, 1979
   This lyrical journey through the seasons with a serene and productive nineteenth-century, rural New England family will give your child (and you) a feeling for America's heritage.

People, Peter Spier, Doubleday, 1980
   An incredibly rich, child-friendly resource of information about the diversity of people and cultures. Beautiful and absorbing illustrations beginning with Adam and Eve in the Garden of Eden, then covering all sorts of human complexities since. This is a book your child will spend hours with and learn much from.

Pretzel, Margaret Rey, Scholastic, 1944
   My twenty-one-year-old daughter Jasmine's favorite love story. The tale of a prize-winning dachshund who can't win the heart of the dog across the street. Unimpressed by the physical qualities that others admire, she finally finds something to admire herself. Marriage and family are the ultimate prize in this old-fashioned heartwarming story.

Read-n-Grow Picture Bible, Word Books, 1979

Two thousand pictures (six per page, with a sentence or two under each) will take your child through the Bible from start to finish. My children have loved this motivational format, which has reinforced the historical continuity of the Bible.

St. Jerome and the Lion, Margaret Hodges, Orchard Books, 1991

Jerome, the medieval monk who lived in Bethlehem and translated the Bible into Latin, earns the devotion of a lion by removing a thorn from his paw. When the monastery's donkey is stolen, the other monks accuse the lion of having eaten it, but only Jerome refuses to condemn him, and is proven right.

The Story about Ping, Marjorie Flack, Viking Press, 1933

A lilting and funny story about a little duck who lives with his comically large family on a boat on the Yangtze River in China. One day while searching for food, he finds himself left behind. Bravely, he goes in search of his family, finding many adventures along the way.

The Story of Babar, Jean De Brunhoff, Random House, 1931

This book, originally written in French, has delighted children and adults for decades. The story of an elephant who loses his mother to hunters, wanders to the city, buys a new wardrobe, becomes the hit of society, marries Celeste, and is crowned King of the Elephants.

The Story of Ferdinand, Munro Leaf, Scholastic, 1936
    One of the best-selling children's books of all time, about a peaceful bull who would rather sit beneath a tree smelling flowers than fight in the bull ring.

William Tell, Margaret Early, Harry N. Abrams, 1991
    A story of courage and purpose. The fourteenth-century Swiss folk hero is forced to shoot an apple from his son's head by the evil governor, then leads his countrymen into action against Austria's tyranny. Still, a man who thinks of himself more as a husband and father than a hero.

The Year at Maple Hill Farm, Alice and Martin Provensen, Aladdin, 1978
    A year in the country with all its seasonal changes—the work, play, and rewards of life on a farm.

EARLY READERS

Bob Books for Beginning Readers (Sets 1, 2, and 3), Bobby Lynn Maslen, Bob Book Publications, 1994.
    These wonderful first phonetic readers will give your child a bridge from reading single words to reading real books. Reading these will reinforce phonetic skills, introduce capital letters, periods, and important sight words, and most importantly, will build his confidence. "Hey, I'm reading a book!"

Step into Reading Books, Various titles and authors, Random House

Over one hundred fun and friendly early readers, divided into four reading levels.

I Can Read Books, Various titles and authors, Harper Trophy

A little more complex (and longer) than the books in the Step into Reading series, these are a good follow-up.

A Beka Books, First Grade Readers

I have used all of these with my children. They are old-fashioned and wholesome. The stories do more than flex the child's reading muscles, they help build character. Each story is followed by comprehension questions, which will train your child to listen to what he is reading, thus helping him become a better learner.

HAPPY ENDINGS

Shortly before I started work on this book, we moved to a house in the country with seven bedrooms. I lined the walls of one with bookshelves and put my desk and computer on one side, two loveseats on the other. As I have written, my children have wandered in and out for books, sprawling across the loveseats and on the floor to read them. When it came time to share my recommendations, I simply went through our shelves and pulled the books I *knew* were the most loved and read in the twenty-eight years since I've been a mother and teacher.

Now I'm sitting in the midst of a tempting array of our very favorite books, thinking that because I've been so busy writing it's been a while since I've read most of them. Also, I've discovered that some of the ones I read a gazillion times to my older children have somehow been overlooked with the younger ones. I've realized that I now have a whole new generation of children to enjoy these books with again.

I'm pretty excited. Excited not only because I've completed a book that will enable me to share the reading approach that's worked so well for our family, but excited because I've been reminded of some wonderful books—that I'll now have a lot more time to read!

But since every story has to have an ending, what ever happened to Allison and Steve? Well, the same thing that happens to most people with one child:

Allison wanted Steve to be surprised when it happened, so she hadn't said anything. Instead, she'd bought the drugstore test and taken it just a day after she'd missed. There was the little pink line! It seemed like a miracle that she could want to have a baby, and then end up being pregnant just like that—especially because the first one seemed to have taken forever.

So, once more they were watching Allison's belly growing round and firm, feeling the baby move, singing and talking to the newest member of the family. Sometimes Tina even read her favorite books aloud to the baby as she snuggled against her mama's side, vowing to continue reading every night to her brother (she said it had to be a boy) for the rest of her life. Allison felt so good about how things were going and how their family was growing.

Yes, indeed, the happiest ending of all—another small beginning!

Appendix A
Magazines

Magazines can stimulate reading in children who might be reluctant to tackle a whole book. (Sound like any adults you know?) Think of magazines as a *positive* resource to get your child hooked on reading, to open vistas to other cultures, classes, and concerns. Encourage your child to share—perhaps at the dinner table—what she has learned from the articles she has read. Here are the best in children's magazines.

Focus on the Family Clubhouse (ages 8–12) and *Clubhouse Jr.* (ages 4–8)

Monthly 24-page Christian magazine filled with articles and stories relevant to kids' lives.

Yearly subscription: $15 and $12. Call 800-232-6459.

God's World

Weekly paper, published in five editions—kindergarten through junior high—featuring current events from a Christian perspective.

Yearly subscription: $19.95. Call 800-951-5437.

Guideposts for Kids (ages 7-12)

Bimonthly 32-page values-based magazine specializing in issue-oriented features and true adventure stories.

Yearly subscription: $15.95. Call 800-431-2344.

Highlights For Kids (ages 2-12)

Monthly 42-page magazine, chock-full of stories, games, and puzzles that get your child used to thinking logically. Yes, it's the same one you may have read when you were a child, and it still appeals to kids!

One-year subscription: $29.64; 3 years: $60.12. Call 800-255-9517.

Kids Discover (ages 6-12, but older kids and parents will enjoy it too!)

Ten issues a year, each devoted to a specific topic, such as ancient China, royalty, Washington, D.C. Beautifully illustrated and full of interesting facts.

One-year subscription: $19.95. Call 800-825-2821.

Sports Illustrated for Kids (ages 8 and up)

Monthly magazine guaranteed to get even the balkiest child reading—as long as he or she loves sports!

One-year subscription: $27.95. Call 800-826-0083.

Be good stewards with magazines. Pass them on to school libraries or hospitals with pediatric units.

Appendix B
Scripture

There is nothing like some words of wisdom from the Bible to put things in perspective. Try these when you're feeling discouraged with the task of parenting.

Trust in the LORD with all your heart
and lean not on your own understanding;
in all your ways acknowledge Him,
and He will make your paths straight.

PROVERBS 3:5–6, NKJV

The end of a matter is better than its beginning,
and patience is better than pride.

ECCLESIASTES 7:8

But those who hope in the LORD
will renew their strength.
They will soar on wings like eagles;
they will run and not grow weary,
they will walk and not be faint.

ISAIAH 40:31

I can do everything through him
who gives me strength.

PHILIPPIANS 4:13

Let us not become weary in doing good,
for at the proper time we will reap a harvest
if we do not give up.

GALATIANS 6:9

Casting all your care upon Him;
for He careth for you.

1 PETER 5:7, KJV

So do not throw away your confidence;
it will be richly rewarded.
You need to persevere so that
when you have done the will of God,
you will receive what he has promised.

HEBREWS 10:35–36

If any of you lacks wisdom, he should
ask God, who gives generously
to all without finding fault, and
it will be given to him.

JAMES 1:5

Appendix C
Red Flags

While there is a considerable range in the time it takes different children to reach language milestones, there are delays that are serious enough to require extra help.

A professional evaluation is recommended if

- you have difficulty understanding your child's speech;
- others have difficulty understanding him;
- your child has difficulty understanding others;
- your child seems uncomfortable with his speech;
- others tease him about the way he talks;
- his voice sounds hoarse or in any way very different from others his age.

Referrals for evaluations can be obtained from your pediatrician, your hospital's speech and hearing clinic, or a speech specialist in the public school system.

If you do suspect a problem, try to keep on an even keel until the information is all in. And even if some type of early intervention is recommended, don't panic. In a couple of years your child may be completely caught up with his peers—whether or not he receives speech and language services. There is considerable debate around the effectiveness of early intervention for nondisabled children with moderate speech delays. As Grover Whitehurst, a specialist in language delays, asserts, "It can get them talking a lot faster, but after a couple years you can't tell the difference between kids who had early intervention and those who did not."[11]

Appendix D
Rethinking TV: A Worn-Out Welcome

Ever had a guest you wish you hadn't invited? Maybe you were looking forward to a little fun and found a lot of wasted time instead.

If so, maybe you'll tune right in to this picture of an ungracious guest.

He plants himself squarely in the room. An attention grabber, he must be easily seen and heard by all who enter.

But a little attention never seems to be enough; it seems like he is always demanding more. He monopolizes every conversation. His friends find it difficult, if not impossible, to get a word in edgewise.

His voice is too loud; his manners, pathetic. He swears and takes God's name in vain. He has little respect for family ties, pokes fun at things that matter deeply, and tells off-color jokes you wish your children hadn't heard.

And yet, he's one of the most popular guests in town—despite his bad manners—invited back again and again. His calendar is full—throughout the day, in the evening, on weekends, in rain or shine, in sickness or in health.

He doesn't discriminate. You'll find him in the homes of the poorest as well as the richest, the happy and the miserable, among all ages, races, and colors.

Maybe you've spent some time with this ill-mannered guest yourself. Maybe sometimes you wish you hadn't.

Somehow the time you spend together seems to mix up your priorities. You find words coming out of your mouth that weren't there before. You find yourself being sarcastic or mean to others in your family. You find yourself distracted by thoughts when you've set a higher standard for your future.

So why do you keep turning on the tube?

Good question, considering that in the United States children watch an average of twenty-one to twenty-seven hours of television per week. An even better question, considering what they're watching.

The American Psychological Association was concerned enough about television's effect on society to form a task force to study and report on their findings.

Their conclusion? The average child watching two to four hours of television a day will have witnessed at least eight thousand murders and one hundred thousand other acts of violence before graduating from elementary school.

What are the effects of watching all this violence? Is it harmless, as some people say? If it's harmful, how can harmfulness be measured?

Many studies have been done, on adults and children, to discover the effects of viewing violence. Here is one example: one hundred preschool children participated by watching twenty to thirty minutes of television three times a week for four weeks. Half the children watched cartoons that had a lot of violence in them; half watched shows with no violence.

Only four to six hours of viewing were spread out over a month. And yet at the end of the month the researchers found a clear difference between the two groups of children.

Those who watched the violent cartoons were more likely to hurt others, argue, and disobey than those who watched non-violent programs. This study was conducted at Pennsylvania State University, and it is typical of studies done throughout the country.

The scientific evidence is conclusive: television violence makes viewers more prone to aggressive behavior in real life.

So, you may be thinking, *I stay away from the violent shows*. Well, what about sex, what about crude jokes, what about sarcasm and meanness and put-downs of others? If viewing violence leads to violence, then surely sitcoms driven by low standards drag down our own.

While some may dispute the influence of television on our daily lives, advertisers don't. They're so convinced of the power of television to mold our thoughts and behavior that they spend billions each year on commercials.

Along these lines, were you aware that movies are filled with subtle and not-so-subtle ads? That familiar candy bar on the table was no coincidence. Hershey's or Nestle's paid to have it there. If the hero picks it up, that means the advertiser paid big bucks. If he actually takes a bite, they paid megabucks.

Advertisers know those dollars are well spent. If the star of the show does it, chances are we will do it too.

And so, for someone who watches a lot of television, there is a question, "How much of who you are is who you really are—the person God meant you to be? And how much is who you've become because of what you've been watching?" For anyone who's not sure of the answer to that question, TV has become more than just an annoyance, it's a menace.

He's like a friend who's worn out his welcome. Even if he doesn't spill his drink or drop crumbs, he's still a guest who leaves a mess behind.

I've included the above article that I've published elsewhere in an effort to put TV in perspective. Each family needs to make an informed decision about TV—to make sure they are controlling its use rather than having it control them.

Our family had no television until the summer of 1996 when we got one of those small satellite dishes to bring in channels that offered some educational value—history and science and art. I still don't allow my children to watch major network sitcoms, mostly because I don't like the crude remarks and sarcastic manner modeled there. I think it's because of lack of exposure that my children usually speak respectfully and with kindness to others.

That's something worth thinking about.

One alternative to television I *heartily* recommend is the *Odyssey* audio series produced by Focus on the Family. These programs can be heard on radio (check your local Christian station for times), or cassette tapes may be purchased from Focus on the Family (800-232-6459). The series is full of highly entertaining, thought-provoking stories with rich vocabulary and historical references. My children have listened to the tapes over and over. Audio programs offer a distinct advantage. While television shows promote passivity, radio or tape programs encourage the child's brain to become actively engaged in creating the story, because the child's imagination is required to supply the "visual."

Appendix E
Where to Find Books

www.amazon.com

They call themselves The Earth's Biggest Bookstore—and you don't have to step outside your door to browse. For those on the Internet, this is an efficient way to buy books—when you know what you want. Search by title or author, find the discounted price, and add to your cyber shopping cart. I have never failed to find a book listed here.

Christian Book Distributors
Call 508-977-5050

Great Christian Books

These are booksellers by mail. Call 800-775-5422 for their catalogs. Discounted prices.

Scholastic Book Clubs

A monthly offering of books, some at big discounts. They are set up as class handouts for different grade levels. Call 800-724-6527 for a teacher's catalog; share brochures with friends; then place an order together.

God's World Book Club

Operates just like Scholastic, only the selection of books is more traditional and Christian. Call 800-951-2665 for a catalog.

A Beka Books

A good starting place for anyone considering home schooling, this ministry provides curriculum for preschool through twelfth grade. Check them out for early readers with wholesome, values-based stories, as well as for language workbooks. Call 800-874-3592 for a catalog.

Appendix F
Stuttering

Most experts agree a stutter that settles in to become a disability is caused by the parent's overreaction to it. Stuttering runs in families because parents who stutter often panic when they hear it in their own children. Parents who are overly conscious of their child's speech will often create the problem they so desperately want to prevent. In speech, easy does it usually works best.

How to Stymie a Stutter

- Listen to *what* your child is saying rather than to *how* he is saying it.
- Don't rush him.
- Don't finish his sentences.
- Don't tell him to slow down or to stop.
- Don't worry yourself or pressure him.
- Act as though the stutter is not there.
- Share these guidelines with everyone close to your child.
- Relax.
- Pray.

Prayer helps enormously. Whether or not prayer takes the stutter away immediately, it will help you relax.

If after six weeks of this minimizing approach your child's speech has not begun to return to normal, ask your pediatrician for a referral to a speech therapist.

Appendix G
Make Your Own Sandpaper Letters

(ONLY IF YOU WANT TO!)

You will need extra-thick, heavy poster board or something similar cut into 5"x7" rectangles.

Paint or cover the board with pink contact paper for consonants, blue for vowels.

Cut letters (remember, only lowercase) from fine sandpaper.

Use rubber cement to glue sandpaper letters onto board, being careful to align the letter $3/4$ inch from the right side of the rectangle. This placement leaves an empty space on the left where the child will place his left hand while tracing the letter with his right, just as we steady a piece of paper with one hand while writing with another.

Optional: Place a red dot on each letter to remind your child where to begin tracing.

Other letter sets available: Felt letters from Beckley-Cardy (see appendix J), $9.95.

Smaller-sized sandpaper letters from Beckley-Cardy (I haven't held these in my hands, but from the picture in the catalog, they look perfect!), $24.95.

Appendix H
Correct Letter Formation

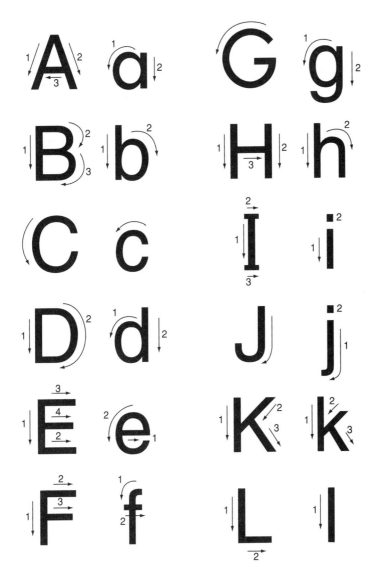

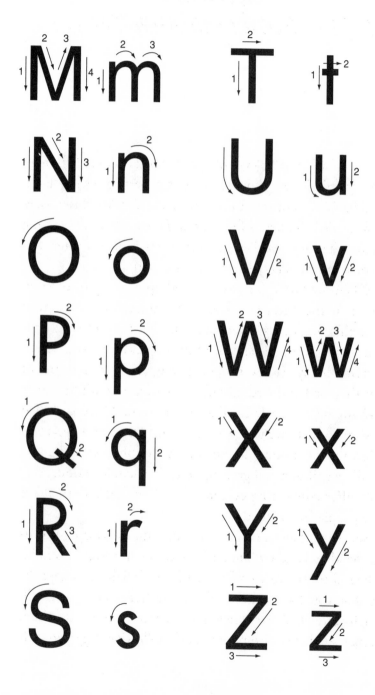

Appendix I
Lefties Need a Little More Thought

As a right-handed parent of right-handed children (although my little Jesse is showing signs of preferring his left hand, as did his birth mother), I had not much considered the issues of left-handed children before writing *Ready, Set, Read!* In trying to anticipate all the challenges a parent might face, I wanted to pass on as much as I could for parents of lefties.

When my library research turned up nothing to pass on, I went to the Internet, found the newsgroup for lefties (alt.lefthanders) and asked the real experts—lefties themselves (some 10 to 13 percent of the population)—for input. I received many replies, some detailing real horror stories of what they had endured as children because of adults intent on changing their left-handed orientation. These included physical punishment as well as humiliation and isolation within the classroom. These stories, coupled with the fact that these children still grew up to be left-handed adults, certainly offer convincing evidence that God did indeed make some people left-handed.

So, if you have encouraged your child to grasp with his right hand by handing him rattles and spoons toward his right, yet he still consistently prefers his left, don't fight it. Accept the fact that you have a lefty. If you are left-handed yourself, though you will already know much about how to teach him, you may still benefit from some of the following suggestions. If you are right-handed, you will definitely need a crash course in translating the learning-to-write process for your child.

To teach a lefty, a left-handed parent should sit to the right and model the left-handed position. Many on the Internet felt that their own right-handed parents and teachers had been most effective when seated across from them in a mirror position. One man said that in spite of many lessons at shoe tying he never "got it" until he happened to come into the room when his mother was tying her own shoes. Fascinated, he watched from the "mirror position," then was finally able to repeat the process on his own shoes.

The best writing position for a lefty would be the reverse of that for a right-handed person. The paper should be tilted to the right, with the bottom right-hand corner angled toward the chest. Encourage your child to hold the pencil so that his hand is not curving up over the top. (Although some lefties do this, many resist this tendency to avoid smearing their writing.) The immediate problem then becomes how to anchor the paper. Since we write left to right, if the right hand anchors the paper on the right side, it will be in the way of the writing. The solution seems to be to bring the right arm over the top of the paper and anchor the top left corner with the right hand. (See illustration on page 160.)

But there is more involved to complicate the writing process for lefties. Our letters are really formed with a left-to-right orientation. None of the online lefties who responded were completely happy with their handwriting. Some had opted for printing, especially all capitals. In teaching left-handed children to write, avoid holding a standard for them that they cannot achieve. Avoid clinging rigidly to the "correct" letter formation process. It may be too difficult for a left-handed child to write a certain letter the way we teach it. For example, insisting that *t*s be crossed from left to right creates more difficulty for a left-handed child. This is one area where the results—consistently readable handwriting and hopefully enjoyment of the writing process—are more important than the details of the process.

I was also advised by lefties to ask parents to advocate for their left-handed children when they go to school: three ring binders are out for lefties. Spiral notebooks are as well, unless the teacher can agree to let them write on the back of the pages as though they were the front.

Appendix J
Helps

My Favorite Workbooks:

Merrill Phonics Skilltext Series—for phonetic skills, verb tenses, plurals, alphabetizing, etc.

- Level R: reading readiness
- Level A: beginning readers
- Levels B-F: as child progresses

Merrill Reading Skilltext—for reading comprehension, study skills, etc.

- *Going Places*: reading readiness
- *Bibs, Mack, Joy*: sequential beginning readers

To order, call 800-843-8855

Teaching Supply Catalogs

Beckley-Cardy
   A humongous (1,300-page) catalog of teaching supplies, from tables and chairs to rhythm instruments to early childhood educational equipment. A great resource. 800-446-1477.

The Sycamore Tree
   A family-run business with more Christian home school books and materials. 714-650-4466.

Endnotes

INTRODUCTION

1. I am convinced that, as with others who came to the Lord later in life, my own early years were not in vain. God's purposes were working themselves out so that all might be in place when the time came for us prodigals to use our talents for his service. I believe my early training was part of God's plan for my life. Whereas some individuals wonder whether the Montessori method is compatible with Christianity, I affirm the validity *only* of Maria Montessori's insights into childhood development and the techniques she developed to increase the child's capacity to learn. Most importantly, the ideas I share have been sifted through what I know to be true as a Christian and are compatible with our faith.

CHAPTER 2

2. Exasperating as spills and accidents can be, parents need to understand what's motivating their child before punishing. When a child spills because she is trying to pour her own milk, for example, she is acting out of her growing need for self-reliance. This should never be confused with bad behavior.

"Lemme doowit myself!" is a cry that actually springs from the child's God-given potential for independence. When we understand that the drive to do things themselves is normal and healthy, then we can allow children opportunities to keep growing in self-reliance skills. This means that if your child wants to pour her own milk, you can show her how to do it by aiming the spout directly over the glass, then holding the handle with the one hand while steadying it underneath with the other.

Each time you break down a task into doable steps, you give your child a gift. You not only provide a positive outlet for his drive for independence, you also show your confidence in his growing abilities.

For more information on how to help your child reach his God-given potential in this area and others, see my book *Small Beginnings, First Steps to Prepare Your Child for Lifelong Learning.*

3. As a Christian, I have found that through God's grace I am not bound by my past. Having come from a troubled background, I made a decision when my first daughter was born to become the kind of mother I would like to have had. I read a lot. I observed other mothers and picked the best as role models. I trusted God to bring out the best in me.

Not only my children have benefited from this, in a way I didn't foresee, I did as well. Becoming a better mother has been enormously healing. I look at it this way: you can't go back and give yourself a happy childhood, but you can provide one for someone else. Jesus calls to us in Matthew 5:48: "Therefore you shall be perfect, just as your Father in heaven is perfect" NKJV.

My message to you then is this: If you came from a wonderful background, being a terrific mother or father will probably come naturally to you. If you didn't, take heart from me. With God's help you can become the kind of parent you want to be.

4. Toni S. Gould, *Get Ready to Read: A Practical Guide for Teaching Young Children at Home and in School* (New York: Walker & Co., 1991), 33.

5. I have home schooled my children for the past eight years, with the exception of six months when I enrolled all but one in a Christian elementary school while I was writing *Small Beginnings.* But after spending last year learning together at home, we are headed for changes again. That's because last summer when we moved to a rural community with a small one-school district, I felt compelled by God to enroll three of my elementary age children in the local public school. I think it's a way for us to become an active ingredient (salt?) in the community. My oldest son, Joshua, will be entering ninth grade at a well-respected Catholic high school, because this seems best suited for him and his future goals. This will leave babies Daniel and Jesse, four-year-old Madeleine, nine-year-old Zachary (who because of his high IQ doesn't fit into school at all), and twelve-year-old Matthew at home with Mom.

    This decision is for this year only. Next summer we will seek God's will for each of the children once again.

    All by way of saying; home schoolers can become legalistic, trapped in the intellectual and spiritual rut of believing home school to be best for all children at all times—no exceptions allowed. I disagree. Home schooling is a decision you make year by year, even moment by moment, after much prayer and seeking God's will for each child. We all need to be careful never to judge another parent's decision.

6. The Christian approach to service means that all our gifts and talents have value only in so far as they are useful to others. Help your child develop this attitude early on. Rather than trying to build his confidence through pride in his own achievements, help him build self-esteem through service to others.

7. Down syndrome is a condition occurring in one out of every eight hundred children in which an extra chromosome is found on the twenty-first pair (hence the name, Trisomy 21). Though limited in intelligence, these children—especially when raised in loving, supportive homes—can grow to be actively contributing members of society, with their own unique gifts to offer. As the mom of three sons with Down Syndrome (one by birth, two by adoption), I know emphatically that Down Syndrome is not an unhappy ending, just the beginning of a different kind of story.

8. I use the term *differently-abled* rather than *disabled* not out of any reactionary political correctness but because it seems the most accurate way to reflect how we appear in God's eyes. Fanny Crosby, a great hymn writer blind from infancy, did not "see" with her physical eyes all that we do, yet she could "see" things in the spiritual realm few are privileged to see. In the past five years since Jonny's birth, as I have pondered my relationships with those with "disabilities," prior to becoming the mother of one, I feel that in God's eyes I may have actually been the disabled one.

9. I must admit, and by now you must have noticed, what an unusual position God has placed me in. As I write this book, most of my friends my age have already finished planning weddings or sending their children off to college. They are dealing with empty-nest syndrome and entering the next season of their lives.

   On the other hand, although I also have one married daughter and three glorious grandchildren—as well as a daughter who will walk down the aisle shortly after this book is finished—I still have nine children under fifteen.

   And so I have another set of women friends, most young enough to be my daughters, with children my children play with. Although I wish I had the energy of the young mothers I know, I am grateful that God has blessed me with being a mother who's in it for the long haul. I am grateful not only for the wisdom he has given me to share but also for the daily hands-on experience he has provided so I can keep in touch with what it's like to be a mother—running after toddlers, changing diapers, making bottles, listening to new readers stumbling over the tricky words. I am so grateful that he has filled my life with young mothers to remind me who I write for!

10. Maria Montessori called this period of childhood "The Absorbent Mind" for good reason. During the preschool years, a child can pick up an amazing number of words that most adults would think too difficult for them. In Montessori classrooms, standard materials include cards of different animal species: birds, reptiles, fish, mammals, and amphibians. The children are taught the names of these in Three Period Lessons during group or individual work time. As a teacher, I was amazed at how eagerly the children listened to and absorbed the names of animals I had never heard of before. At their age, the desire to master any knowledge of the world within their reach is so strong that until you have seen it, it would be hard to believe.

11. "When a Child's Silence Isn't Golden," *Newsweek*, Special Issue on Child Development, (spring 1997): 23.

Bibliography

The following books were used to research and validate my own experience and observations of the language development/reading process.

Beadle, Muriel. *A Child's Mind: How Children Learn during the Critical Years from Birth to Age Five.* Garden City, New York: Doubleday and Company, 1970.

Gould, Toni S. *Get Ready to Read: A Practical Guide for Teaching Young Children at Home and in School.* New York: Walker & Co., 1991.

Lattman, Michelle, and Antoinette Seandel. *Better Speech for Your Child.* New York: Weyden Books, 1977.

Warner, Silas, M.D., and Edward B. Rosenberg. *Your Child Learns Naturally: What Can You Do to Help Prepare Your Child for School?* Garden City, New York: Doubleday and Company, 1976.

Weiner, Harvey S. *Talk with Your Child: How to Develop Reading and Language Skills through Conversation at Home.* New York: Viking, 1988.